UNDER HIMMLER'S COMMAND

The Personal Recollections of
Oberst Hans-Georg Eismann, Operations
Officer, Army Group Vistula,
Eastern Front 1945

Helion WWII German Military Studies Volume 2

Oberst Hans-Georg Eismann
Translated and edited by Frederick P. Steinhardt, MS, PhD.

Helion & Company Ltd

Also in this series:
Volume 1   *Panzer Lehr Division 1944-45* (ISBN 9781874622284 hardback; ISBN 9781906033521 paperback)

Helion & Company Limited
26 Willow Road
Solihull
West Midlands
B91 1UE
England
Tel. 0121 705 3393
Fax 0121 711 4075
Email: info@helion.co.uk
Website: www.helion.co.uk

Published by Helion & Company 2010

Designed and typeset by Farr out Publications, Wokingham, Berkshire
Cover designed by Farr out Publications, Wokingham, Berkshire
Printed by The Cromwell Press Group, Trowbridge, Wiltshire

This English edition © Helion & Company Limited 2009. Translated and edited by Frederick P. Steinhardt, MS, PhD.

Front cover photograph: A command conference with Hitler at the HQ of *Heeresgruppe 'Weichsel'*, early March 1945. Hitler is in conversation with (far right) *General der Infanterie* Theodor Busse, CO *9. Armee*. (Bundesarchiv 146-1971-033-33). Rear cover photograph: *Generaloberst* Gotthard Heinrici (right), commander of *Heeresgruppe 'Weichsel'* 21 March-29 April 1945. This image was taken in September 1943, when Heinrici was CO 4. *Armee*. (Bundesarchiv 146-1977-120-09)

Maps originally appeared in Earl F. Ziemke's *Stalingrad to Berlin: the German Defeat in the East* (Washington, DC: US Army Center of Military History, 1968). Due acknowledgement is hereby given to the copyright holders.

ISBN 978 1 874622 43 7

British Library Cataloguing-in-Publication Data.
A catalogue record for this book is available from the British Library.

For details of other military history titles published by Helion & Company Limited contact the above address, or visit our website: http://www.helion.co.uk.

We always welcome receiving book proposals from prospective authors.

Contents

List of Maps

Maps originally appeared in Earl F. Ziemke's *Stalingrad to Berlin: the German Defeat in the East* (Washington, DC: US Army Center of Military History, 1968). Due acknowledgement is hereby given to the copyright holders.

Translator's Note

Oberst i. G. Eismann's notes on his service under *Reichsführer-SS* Heinrich Himmler with Army Group Vistula (hereinafter rendered as *Heeresgruppe Weichsel*) have never before been published in any language. Due to his unusual position, as a regular army officer with general staff training and experience under Himmler, who was not qualified to command an army group, Eismann was not only called upon to exceed the usual scope of his position as Operations Officer, but was also a trained observer of very significant and unusual events (see Foreword). Because this publication makes available for the first time in published form an important historical document, the style of translation is appropriate for scholarly use, even though, at times, this may interfere slightly with general readability.

German military documents usually refer to specific maps. Place names are spelled precisely as on the particular map referred to, even if misspelled or incorrect. That permits accurate location on that map of geographical references. A different document may use a different map. In some cases, that map may have different names or spellings for the identical locations. In informal translation it is customary to standardize geographical references. If a translation is to be used for research purposes, it is important to preserve the original geographical references. Similarly, factual errors in the original document should be preserved, as such.

In translating *Oberst i.G.* Eismann's notes, except as noted below, all place names are given as he gave them. Where they are not immediately obvious, a modern equivalent is presented in brackets on the first appearance. Exception has been made in the case of countries, seas, a few large geographical entities and German provinces (such as Hungary rather than *Ungarn*, Crimea rather than *Krim*, Baltic Sea rather than *Ostsee*, West Prussia rather than *Westpreußen* and Pomerania rather than *Pommern*. Rivers retain their German names. The translator must admit to and apologize for occasional inconsistencies and personal idiosyncrasies resulting, in part, from such long immersion in German accounts that he sometimes forgets that there are English geographical designations that differ from the German. In some cases I was unable to match pre-war place names in Pomerania and the sections in eastern Germany which are now Poland with the modern Polish names.

Due to the general unfamiliarity of this sector of the war to modern readers, the editor/translator has taken the liberty of inserting extensive notes. All material in square brackets was inserted by the translator/editor. All footnotes were also inserted by the editor/translator except those specifically identified as 'author's footnote'.

Military unit abbreviations have generally been expanded and standardized as per Tessin[1] for regular army, and Bender[2] for SS. Upon first occurrence the original

---

1   Tessin, Georg, *Verbände und Truppen der deutschen Wehrmacht und Waffen SS im Zweiten Weltkrieg 1939 – 1945*, Osnabrück, Biblio Verlag, 1974, 2. Auflage, 18 volumes.
2   Bender, Roger James and Hugh Page-Taylor, *Uniforms, Organization and History of the Waffen-SS*, San Jose CA, R. James Bender Publishing, 1969, 5 volumes.

abbreviation and unit designation is given as presented by *Oberst i.G.* Eismann in brackets. All subsequent mentions follow Tessin and Bender.

I retain the German *Abteilung* for cavalry, artillery and armoured commands rather than replacing it with the English 'battalion', only using 'battalion' where the German usage is '*Bataillon*'. I have, in many cases, employed the somewhat cumbersome English term, 'armoured fighting vehicles' rather than 'tanks' when the reference included both tanks and assault guns (*Sturmgeschütze*). In general, those German terms that are retained are always given as nominative and the German plural is used.

In a few cases I have given the original German term in brackets and continued to do so where it seemed that it might be helpful to some readers who are accustomed to seeing the untranslated German term, as, for example 'command section [*Führungsabteilung*]' of the *Heeresgruppe* command.

Editor's Foreword

*O*berst *i.G.* Eismann's assignment as *Ia* (Operations Officer) to *Heeresgruppe 'Weichsel'* was unique in that he was a regular army officer, trained for general staff work (as signified by the abbreviation, *i.G., im Generalstab*) assigned to *Heeresgruppe 'Weichsel'*, commanded by *Reichsführer-SS* Heinrich Himmler, one of Hitler's closest cronies at that time, a man greatly feared as the head of the *Waffen-SS* and *Gestapo*, but with no training or qualifications at all for military command. Indeed, *Oberst i.G.* Eismann's account describes an event unique in military history: an Army Group activated to take charge of a critical situation, a military disaster in the making; its Commander-in-Chief a total lay person, the hastily assembled and heterogeneous staff provided with neither materiel nor personnel to command or control large bodies of troops.

As the crisis deepened, *Reichsführer* Himmler took to his sick-bed, essentially unavailable for decisions, recovering almost instantly upon his relief and replacement by *Generaloberst* Heinrici. *Oberst i.G.* Eismann's account of service under *Generaloberst* Heinrici bears witness to the outstanding personal, moral and military qualities of this upright and capable man who was a shining example of the best of the Prussian tradition, a true gentleman and soldier. Eismann was there when Heinrici put his career and his life on the line, issuing orders to save the men of his *Heeresgruppe*, defying Hitler's express orders.

Oberst i.G. Eismann also tells how *General* von Tippelskirch briefly filled in, commanding *Heeresgruppe 'Weichsel'* until *General* Student arrived, too late to control and not even to be present at the *Heeresgruppe's* final fragmented surrender.

Oberst i.G. Eismann provides insights regarding the personalities, their interaction and functioning as the *Heeresgruppe* command interacted with armies (*Armeen*) and corps (*Korps*) and with OKH, OKW and Hitler himself. *Oberst i.G.* Eismann's account is unselfconscious, totally devoid of self-justification, bearing witness to his own personal stature as an honourable soldier, officer and gentleman under all circumstances.

Unfortunately it has not been possible to locate a photograph of *Oberst i.G.* Eismann.

Introductory Letters[1]

CMH (25 April 57)
Subject: Aufzeichnungen Oberst i. G. Eismann als Ia der Heeresgruppe 'Weichsel'
Dept of the Army, Office of the Chief of Military History, Washington 25, D.C.
Corrections as per letter dtd 5 March 1957, Subject: Aufzeichnungen Oberst i.G.
Eismann als Ia der Heeresgruppe 'Weichsel'. Inserted 25 April 1957. A copy of this letter
is attached to the original manuscript D-408.

(signed)
MAGNA E. BAUER

⌇

HEADQUARTERS
Capt Sawyer/ba
UNITED STATES ARMY, EUROPE
Historical Division
APO 164
New York, NY
5 March 1957
AEAHI 314.7/1
SUBJECT: Aufzeichnungen Oberst i. G. Eismann als Ia der Heeresgruppe 'Weichsel'
TO: Chief, Military History
            Department of the Army
            Washington 25, D. C.

1. Reference letters, your office, dated 29 January 1957, and this office, dated 20 February 1957.

2. The following data have been obtained from Generalleutnant a.D. Ferdinand Heim, for inclusion in MS # D-408:

PAGE	MISSING INFORMATION[2]
74	30 January
76	25 January
91	15 February
97	14 February
99	15 February
112	3 March
134	?
135	6 March

---

1   Publishers' note – these letters appear at the beginning of the original manuscript and are included in this publication for the sake of completeness.

2   Translator's note – All of the above data was already entered by hand in the original document.

FOR THE CHIEF, HISTORICAL DIVISION:
(Signed)
EDWARD J. BARTA
Lt Colonel, Infantry
Deputy Chief

Military Biographical Notes on the Author

Oberst i.G. a.D. [*i.G.* = *im Generalstab*, trained for General Staff work; *a.D.* = *außer Dienst*, retired], *Abiturient* [passed final examination for graduation from German secondary schools] 1 April 1927, joined *Infanterie Regiment* 16 [*I. R.* 16] at Oldenburg. In this regiment he was platoon leader, company commander and battalion adjutant.

1937, Regimental Adjutant, *Infanterie Regiment* 74 [*I. R.* 74] at Hameln.

1938/39 *Kriegsakademie* [war college] at Berlin (*Hauptmann*).

1939 at the start of the war as *O1* (First *Ordonnanzoffizier*)1 with *Armeeoberkommando* 5 [*AOK* 5] and *Armeeoberkommando* 18 [*AOK* 18], in Poland and the Western Campaign, respectively.

1940 Transfer to the 260th *Infanterie Division* [260th *Inf. Div.*] as *Ib* (2nd General Staff Officer) [logistics].

At the start of the Eastern Campaign (June 1941) *Ia* of *XXX Armeekorps* (1st General Staff Officer [operations], campaigns in southern Ukraine and Crimea.

May 1942 *Ic* (3rd General Staff Officer [intelligence] *Armeeoberkommando* 11 [*AOK* 11] (*Oberbefehlshaber* [commander in chief] von Manstein).

1942 (November) *Ic Heeresgruppe 'Don'*. Battle of Stalingrad.

1943 (March) 1st General Staff Officer [*Ia*] 297th *Infanterie Division* [297th *Inf. Div.*] employed in Rumania – Albania.

1943 (September) 1st General Staff Officer [*Ia*] *Armeeoberkommando* 6 [*AOK* 6], fighting retreat from Mius river to Dnjester river, fighting in Rumania, retreat to Hungary.

1944 (September) Chief of the liaison staff with the Royal Hungarian Army. Fighting in Hungary.

1944 (December) Transfer to the *Kriegsakademie* as an instructor. This did not take effect.

1945 (end of January or beginning of February) Assignment as 1st General Staff Officer [*Ia*] to *Heeresgruppe 'Weichsel'*, commanded by *Reichsführer SS* Heinrich Himmler. Initial organization of the *Heeresgruppe* staff, final combat of this *Heeresgruppe* in the Posen area, West Prussia, Pomerania and Mecklenburg until the final capitulation. As a result of the unusual command setup of this *Heeresgruppe*, with *Reichsführer SS* as Commander in Chief [*Oberbefehlshaber*] and the Chief of the General Staff, both having little training in the command of large formations, the *Ia* [operations officer] was far more deeply involved in the operational command than was normal.

---

1   Translator's note – The *O1*, first *Ordonnanzoffizier* served as aid to the *O1*, operations officer.

Part I

The author originally inserted a first section (pages 1 to 10) before the pages that follow, in which he included some recollections of a brief portion of his activity at the *Kriegsakademie* and in courses for higher command of troops. In a letter dated 18 December 1956 the author informed *Generalmajor a.D.* Alfred Toppe that he had destroyed that section.

Part II

On 14 or 15 January 1945 I was suddenly informed by the Commander of the Courses for Higher Command of Troops [*Lehrgänge für höhere Truppenführung*] that, effective immediately, I was assigned as First General Staff Officer of *Heeresgruppe 'Weichsel'*. I was to depart that very day for Schneidemühl and my new duties.

Although I was well informed about the organization of our *Heeresgruppen* and armies, this command was entirely new to me. In response to my astonished questions in this regard *General* Brennecke told me that this *Heeresgruppe* had been newly formed to build a new defensive front at the Vistula river between *Heeresgruppe Mitte* [Center] and *Heeresgruppe Nord* [North]. When I inquired as to the Commander in Chief and the Chief of the General Staff, I learned that the Commander in Chief was *Reichsführer-SS* Heinrich Himmler. The Chief of the General Staff was not known but was, in any case, an *SS* general. I was less than overjoyed at the prospect of again being *Ia* [operations officer] and, additionally, more than surprised at the identity of those holding the highest positions in this new command. Although I had long experience and was accustomed to extremely unusual situations, this high command situation was beyond anything I had ever met.

More than anything else, I could not understand just why I had been placed in this extremely high level of command through this appointment as *Ia*. The *P3* (the section of the Army Personnel Bureau [*Heerespersonalamt*] for the General Staff) knew that I was a rather critical subordinate and definitely not imbued with the 'ideas' of National Socialism. Questions of that sort, however, could not be put to the equally astonished *General* Brennecke. With those thoughts churning in my head I drove through the icy winter night in a command car toward a new, unknown and unmistakably dubious fate.

The journey via Frankfurt-an-der-Oder/Küstrin made clear to me the entire extent of the confusion and misery of the homeland that had, hitherto, been entirely unknown to me and, indeed, unsuspected from my duty-stations abroad. Endless processions of refugees from the east lined all highways. Amongst them were *Wehrmacht* vehicles and even troops. It was often unclear which direction the refugee columns were headed. At times these processions passed each other headed in opposite directions. There was a general impression of disorder. The condition of the people and animals in these treks was most deplorable. A refugee column in totally blacked-out and heavily bomb-shattered Frankfurt-an-der-Oder seemed especially hopeless. The air buzzed with countless rumours. All were greatly exaggerated, but one was entirely correct: the Russians were driving inexorably to the west, the Anglo–Americans thrusting eastward toward them.

During the last few weeks the only details I had learned had come through the *Wehrmacht* reports. Experience had shown how much or, rather, how little they provided. I was, therefore, naturally interested in gaining a more-or-less accurate picture of the situation. I was hoping to gain this information at the new *Heeresgruppe*, though I knew from experience how the *Wehrmacht* command, meaning Hitler, left even the highest staffs uninformed.

Reichsführer-SS Heinrich Himmler, first CO of *Heeresgruppe*
'Weichsel'. (Bundesarchiv 146-1976-143-21)

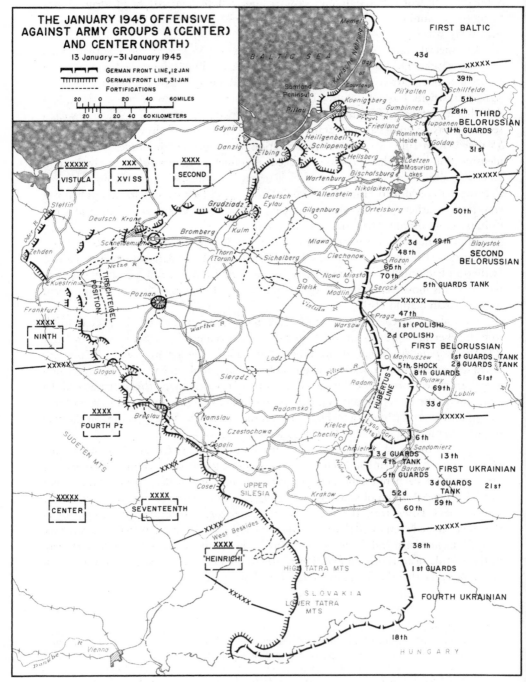

The January 1945 offensive

Upon my arrival in Schneidemühl I inquired at a traffic-control post regarding Staff *'Weichsel'*. Nobody had heard of it. Obviously it was a top-secret affair. At the Schneidemühl Fortress Command Post [*Festungskommandantur*] Schneidemühl was being turned into one of Hitler's ill-fated 'fortresses'[1] – *Major* von Hase, whom I knew personally, was finally able to give me information.

The special train *'Steiermark'* of the *Reichsführer-SS* was at the Deutsch-Krone railroad station. He knew no more than that. Accordingly, I proceeded onward to Deutsch-Krone. I arrived there as darkness fell at about 1730 hours. There too refugees were everywhere. I asked a railroad employee about the *'Steiermark'* train. He replied, *'Ach*, the *Reichsführer-SS's* train is over there.' The matter no longer seemed to be such a secret. It was an endlessly long train of sleeping-cars. At every third car was a *Waffen-SS* sentry with rifle. My only documentation was my marching-order and soldier's identification book. That, however, sufficed. A young *Untersturmführer* received me in an elegant dining car. He said I was already urgently awaited. We went through the long sleeping-car corridor to Himmler's Chief Adjutant, *SS Obersturmführer* Grothmann. I was greeted rather formally by that officer, who was still very young, but held a not-unimportant position. His attitude seemed rather chilly.

After a brief wait I was presented to the new Commander in Chief, *Reichsführer-SS* Heinrich Himmler, a man feared by ordinary mortal Germans, of which I was one. Hitherto I had only known him from a distance and from pictures. I had only a vague picture of his most recent, much discussed, position of power – he was now considered to be the man behind Hitler.

Himmler received me sitting at the desk in his elegant saloon-car. I reported myself to him, whereupon he moved to a large table in the center of the room where an *OKH* [*Oberkommando des Heeres*, Army High Command] situation map was laid out. He asked me several short questions about my previous employment and then went into a very animated sort of briefing about the situation on the map. This map showed the situation on the Eastern Front as of a few days earlier (roughly 15 January 1945.) From the somewhat erratic briefing by Himmler, on the one hand, and the picture on the map, on the other hand, I got the following general picture:

The continuity of the German Eastern Front between *Heeresgruppe 'Mitte'* and *Heeresgruppe 'Nord'* that had been lost as a result of events in the sector of *Heeresgruppe 'Mitte'* had not been re-established.. Apparently there was a deep penetration, if not, indeed, a breakthrough of strategic significance, with its primary direction toward the mid-Vistula – Posen area. The 9th *Armee* of *Heeresgruppe 'Mitte'*, ostensibly fighting in that area, seemed pretty well shattered and scattered. The at-least badly battered southern wing of the northern 2nd *Armee* was hanging in the air about two day's march to the east of the Vistula near Thorn. In addition to the heavy pressure on the front it was clearly apparent to me that the Russians were outflanking our forces.

---

1 Translator's note – When Hitler declared a location a *Festung* (fortress) the officer he appointed as fortress commander received special powers, including the right to commandeer any person or unit coming within the boundaries of his jurisdiction. The 'fortress' could not be evacuated or surrendered without express authorization from Hitler. Frequently Hitler's designation had nothing to do with the defensibility or fortification of the position.

The relationship between the enemy and our own troops in the roughly 120 kilometer broad gap between *Heeresgruppen 'Mitte'* and *'Nord'* was not entirely clear. There no longer appeared to be any combat-worthy large German formations. Command relationships were similarly unclear. Probably there were no communications between the fragmented formations depicted on the map.

The mission of the newly-formed *Heeresgruppe 'Weichsel'* was to re-establish the continuity of the front, advancing it as far to the east as possible and to prevent the Russians from any further advance toward the Baltic coast. That was supposed to establish a combat-worthy defensive front at least along the general line central-Silesia – lower Vistula. The mission was clear and simple on paper. What, however, were the actual prospects for carrying it out? Since, in the course of the Eastern campaigns, I had experienced numerous penetrations and major breakthroughs in operational command situations (Stalingrad – Rumania – Hungary) I was not too greatly shaken by the events and the picture.

I immediately asked, 'With what is this breach to be closed and the new front then to be held?' The entire Eastern campaign had been a war with no reserves, or, at least, no strategic reserves, indeed, usually without tactical reserves. This was an innovation that the 'Greatest *Feldherr* [overall strategic commander] of All Times' had made the norm.[2] Despite outstanding performance on the part of the troops, and, to the extent possible for competent command by the regular military authorities under Hitler's supreme command this innovation had necessarily led from one disaster to another. Accordingly, I feared that in this case, too, adequate reserves were unavailable. Up to this point Himmler had spoken while energetically sweeping the pointer around the map. The quintessence of his rather obscure presentation had, however, been: I shall bring the Russians to a halt with *Heeresgruppe 'Weichsel'*, and then smash them and hurl them back. This was quite a statement. Certainly any great field-commander should strive for the highest objectives with corresponding self-confidence and thereby take upon himself a great deal of responsibility. But a certain level of sound judgement regarding the relevant military questions must go hand-in-hand with this. Here one had the involuntary impression that a blind man was talking of colors. Therefore I simply inquired what forces the *Heeresgruppe* had available for the intended mission. This was the natural question any soldier would ask who was given such a mission. Himmler answered me with some impatience that the 9th and 2nd *Armee*, the fortress troops of Thorn, Graudenz, Posen and several smaller places that I had never suspected to be fortresses, as well as all available troops in the sector of the acting *Generalkommando* XX in Posen were attached to *Heeresgruppe 'Weichsel'*.[3] The attachment of two armies would, generally, give one quite a feeling of confidence. However, think of their condition as described above. The 9th *Armee* was shattered and now consisted of little more than its name. Its current combat effectiveness was hardly known to its own command, let alone

---

2 Translator's note – German propaganda had christened Hitler *'Der größte Feldherr aller Zeiten'* and referred so many times to him as such, that it had become a bitterly derisive reference to him among military men disillusioned by the frequently disastrous results of Hitler's personal intervention in military operations. This 'title' was sometimes abbreviated as *'Grofaz'*.

3 Translator's note – Fortress troops were generally composed of older men, sometimes with health problems. They lacked vehicles and logistical support elements that would be required for mobile operations in the field.

OKH or the *Heeresgruppe*. Realistically considered, it probably had none. At this point there was no way of knowing whether any combat-worthy troops could be gathered and organized from the scattered remnants of this army.

The 2nd *Armee,* under its proven East Prussian commander, *Generaloberst* Weiß, consisted of four *Korps* with a total of about ten divisions. As far as mere numbers went, that was entirely adequate. This army's sector, however, stretched from southeast of Thorn to roughly Deutsch-Eylau, thus approximately over 130 kilometers. Its condition was that of any army that had fought for over a year in the East in extremely difficult defensive combat and fighting retreat. To any experienced soldier that meant that, without going into detail, the divisions were down to about one-third of their normal fighting strength. Even that was only numerical strength. The physical condition of the troops, their matériel and morale were not considered in that statement. These three by-no-means unessential factors for the realistic evaluation of the troops had been left out of Hitler's calculations for years. All he considered were overall numbers and unit designations on the map.

Every month the regular, and often additional irregular, condition reports were sent to *OKH* for every single element or formation of troops. With almost no exceptions, they presented a clear, unvarnished picture of both the overall condition of the troops and the details. No conclusions, however, were drawn from these regarding the combat-readiness and effectiveness of the troops. Apparently these reports were merely collected in some file or, perhaps, set aside for use at some later date in writing a history of the war. The latter would not have been very lucid.

The troops referred to, aside from the two armies, could not have been considered as significant in the operational sense of the mission. Seen in retrospect, they might have had a total collective numerical strength of two to three infantry divisions. Given these facts, it was clear to me that the great gap torn by the penetration remained a breach and that there was no way of fulfilling the *Heeresgruppe* mission unless the Supreme Command provided new forces at the earliest possible time. Therefore I asked Himmler what additional forces would be provided and when.

Instead of an answer I now received from my new Commander in Chief a rather loud and discourteous lecture about my typical general-staff outlook that culminated with the accusation that general-staff officers only had misgivings, they were academically trained, they could not improvise, their attitude was defeatist and so on. He – Himmler – would put an end to such misgivings and attack the situation with ruthless energy. That was the only way in which such difficult situations could be mastered. Already, as Commander in Chief on the Upper Rhine [*Oberbefehlshaber am Oberrhein*]. he had had to dispense with this sort of general-staff outlook.

All of this was, doubtless, correct in so far as any Commander-in-Chief, especially that commander, should make as clear as possible to his subordinates his basic viewpoint. The question remained, however, how this great breach in the front was to be sealed. My only reply to this extensive discourse was that I was, indeed, a general-staff officer and had been assigned to his staff in that capacity. In my previous official positions during the war it had been my duty and assignment to question the Commander-in-Chief and express valid opinions regarding the situation. Only by so doing could I attempt to carry out the assignment I had been given and only by so doing would my presence here serve any useful purpose. Thereupon I was told that the statements concerning the general-staff had been general in nature and were not meant personally. He hoped that we would be able to work well together. We would discuss the situation again the following morning if we had new information about the front.

In response to a final question of mine about the Chief of the General Staff, Himmler stated that he – an *SS Brigadeführer* Lammerding – would arrive in a few days from the West. Until his arrival, I had to serve as acting Chief. No more questions were raised. I was now dismissed in friendly fashion and departed with quite mixed feelings.

It would be natural, at this point, to ask what my first impression of Himmler was. Outwardly he was of medium size, his torso a bit too long, light in the thighs, a bit on the plump side, he wore his usual simple field-gray uniform. Seen face-on, his head was rather like a pointed triangle. His profile was particularly marked by a receding chin. His countenance was very mobile, usually with squinting eyes which, with his cheekbones, gave a slightly Mongolian look. His mouth was narrow, but not cruel. All in all, this broad face was neither demonic, cruel nor in any way remarkable. It was the face of an average citizen. Conspicuous, however, at least for a man who expressed himself with gestures, were his hands. There was nothing noble about them. They were rather plump, without being fat, long-fingered hands with wide finger-tips, soft as a woman's when he shook hands.

In other respects my impression of Himmler was that of a lively man with manifold interests, markedly energetic and determined. At this first encounter there was no way of judging whether he had special talents and knowledge. One thing, however, was obvious: he had no sound military knowledge. Thus, for the first time, I met a high military commander and superior who was lacking all prior experience and foundations for an extremely difficult, purely military assignment.

At risk of going into excessive detail for the non-soldier, I must go a bit further into the organization of the staff of *Heeresgruppe 'Weichsel'*, since, so far as I know, this was probably a unique situation for such an important command staff in previous military history. It was novel to appoint a lay-person to the position of Commander-in-Chief. One would have expected that such a man would have been provided with a command instrument that was flawlessly tuned and, thereby, ready for instant employment. The extremely critical situation demanded no less. Whether a man like Himmler believed he could dispense with such a tool or whether the excessive haste with which this new command had been activated was to blame, the fact remained that the *Heeresgruppe* staff was in no way ready for action. There was, indeed, a fully manned logistical administrative section, but it had no vehicles at all and no logistical troops. Therefore it could neither direct nor carry out on its own the supply of the troops. The command section consisted of three general-staff officers. That was all. There were no *Ordonnanzoffizier* [special-missions staff officers], no clerks, no draftsmen, no typewriters, no vehicles and – what was most critical – no communications equipment other than the telephone of the Chief Adjutant, which I had to share with him. It should be noted as a not-insignificant curiosity that there was only the one outdated situation map that Himmler, himself, had. By chance I had brought with me for the journey a 1:300,000 map. I always kept a few drawing-pencils with me, so at least, I could start with a blank map and roughly enter the rapidly changing situation. I felt like Robinson of the Swiss Family Robinson when he first landed on the island. Even to a complete military layman it would be obvious that one cannot command a military force with the strength of two armies on a roughly 250 kilometer front like a company commander shouting from man to man, even if the entire front was quiet and in order. Here, even that eternally misunderstood and overworked cliché, 'improvisation' failed utterly. To one familiar with the overwhelmingly crucial significance of communications for the higher commands in modern war – telephones, teletypes, radios, aircraft – even the most brilliant improvisor would be stymied if he had essentially nothing in the way of communications equipment available.

Today any higher staff, indeed, every staff in all the armies in the world, includes a communications unit. Its strength and technical capabilities are fitted to the needs of the relevant staff – better said – appropriate to the number of the attached troops and the consequent distances that must be bridged. Thus, a signals platoon is adequate for a battalion. A *Heeresgruppe* requires a signals regiment with 3 – 4 battalions [*Abteilungen*]. Here, however, was neither a signals platoon nor a regiment.

The special train '*Steiermark*' was the mobile, so-called 'Field Command Post' of *Reichsführer-SS* Himmler. He had in it an extremely modern, relatively comfortable instrument to carry out, at least in makeshift fashion, while traveling, his duties as *Reichsführer-SS*, Interior Minister, Police Chief, Commander-in-Chief of the Replacement Army [*Ersatzheer*] and the like. There were, thus, deputies for all the positions mentioned above in this train, each with a small staff of aids, secretaries, typewriters, files and whatever else they required. For communications there was a telephone system, one teletype and one radio station. The so-called staff of the *Heeresgruppe* was now politely directed to this set-up, planned and arranged for completely different tasks. It is hardly necessary to explain that even as an emergency solution for a short time it was impossible to command an army group, working in single room, in which female secretaries and ministry-clerks were working at all conceivable tasks – size: half of a railway car – squatting at the corner of a table, that did not even belong to one, with a telephone that had to be shared simultaneously with ten other people. One might as well have used a public coin-telephone booth.

Accordingly, the first task had to be to put together a makeshift command-instrument out of nothing before any practical influence could be exerted on the course of events. The *OKH*, responsible for the activation of this staff, promised all that was humanly possible. But when could all that arrive? In praiseworthy fashion the *Oberquartiermeister* [Deputy Chief of the General Staff] *Oberst i.G.* von Rücker and the two other general-staff officers, *Oberstleutnant i.G.* Wessel (*Ic*) [intelligence] and *Oberstleutnant* Harnack (*Ia/F*) [operations/command] supported me in this. Without their indefatigable activity it would have been impossible to even make a beginning. It must be kept in mind that the *Ia* [operations officer] of a *Heeresgruppe* who is, at the same time, filling in as Chief of the General Staff, has a tremendous amount of work to do and, actually, has no time to look for typewriters, beg for telephone equipment, come up with map-sheets and run around to various places looking for a vehicle and other important things. The Commander-in-Chief, to whom I presented this impossible situation of the so-called command staff, did, indeed, have a certain understanding of the situation, but, aside from that, he knew so little of the technical side of what was going on that, by order of *OKH*, he wanted to assume command of the 2nd and 9th *Armeen* the following day. I registered a strong protest against this with the warning that so far as command and control went there was no way that one could technically and responsibly take over command of two armies with which there was not one single secure communications link. *OKH* had proposed that, with its assistance, he should assume command over at least one *Armee*, the 2nd. My protest, however, gained only a single day. Then Himmler officially assumed command, even without communications links. His only justification: The *Führer* expects it of me that I will get to work as quickly as possible. Those were approximately Himmler's words when I again explained that actual command would not be possible under the given circumstances until usable communications with the attached armies were established. Even if all the resources of heaven and hell were set in motion, this would take about four days. There was nothing else that could be done. Effective 18 January at 0000 hours Himmler reported assumption of command, thereby taking full responsibility for one of the most critically important sectors of the German Eastern Front. It was only later that the thought occurred to me that, in so doing, right at the beginning of his command *OKH* was already trying to trip Himmler up. There is no other way, even with the extravagant conceptions of our highest military command at that time, that it is imaginable that such a ridiculous action would have been required. Later it will be necessary to return to this point with increasing frequency.

So much for now. The appointment of Himmler to a decisive military command was, first of all, one of those final desperate and unplanned measures of Hitler's to, in some way, change the ever more unbearable military situation. Here was the *idée fixe* to employ one of his most faithful paladins and unconditionally proven tools instead of the hated and defeatist generals. As was so often the case, other technical considerations played no role. However, as time passed, one also gradually gained the impression that the camarilla around Hitler saw here a unique opportunity initially to neutralize one of the most feared and powerful men by sending him to the military sector and, possibly, by so doing to discredit him on this level with his lord and master, for, apparently, everyone except Himmler himself saw that there were no longer any laurels to be gained at this new post of honour. The fact is that Himmler lost heavily in influence. Hitler was seriously disillusioned by the course of the later military events and treated Himmler accordingly. At the very least, Bormann – the 'Gray Eminence' – in the *Führerhauptquartier* [*Führer* headquarters] expected events to follow this course and rubbed his hands in satisfaction.

To the tragicomedy of activation of a capable *Heeresgruppe* staff can finally be added that, two months later, a staff had developed that was fully capable of performing its task and able to meet all challenges. Himmler's successor, *Generaloberst* Heinrici, a long-experienced commander in chief, stated that he had seldom had such a well-functioning staff. That was a splendid recognition for all the men who, along with the urgent central tasks, had formed this instrument with endless care.

Following the over-hasty assumption of command by the *Heeresgruppe,* the situation steadily worsened. It was obvious that, without additional forces, there was no possibility of sealing the gaps on both sides of Posen. Thus the Posen fortress was left to stand as a 'breakwater', to tie down as many enemy forces as possible and provide time for rebuilding a continuous front in the general line Vistula – Netze (south of Schneidemühl) – Oder-Warthe position.

In the meantime Thorn 'opened the dance' for the encircled fortresses in the *Heeresgruppe 'Weichsel'* sector. The Russians showed no concern for these so-called fortresses, simply continuing their advance westward. Thus, after losing all artillery, heavy weapons and vehicles, the garrison of about 25,000 men, along with about twice that number of German refugees, constantly threatened and ambushed by Russians, reached Bromberg about four to five days later after an arduous march. The enemy had put little effort into preventing this retreat. It appeared that he figured that he would be just as able to wipe out the exhausted Thorn garrison after it had arrived in Bromberg along with the Bromberg garrison. This time it was more serious. Bromberg was at the confluence of the Bromberg Canal – thus the Netze river with the Brahe river – and, directly west of the mouth of the Brahe river in the Vistula. Bromberg thereby formed the eastern corner-post of a Brahe – Netze defense. The latter was the natural protection of the deep southern flank of a defense of the lower Vistula. After the loss of Thorn and the realization that the *Heeresgruppe* would, if at all and at the earliest, form a defense on both sides of Posen to prevent a further Russian advance, this flank protection was built by the 2nd *Armee* with hastily thrown-together makeshift forces.

The strategic intentions of the Russian command against *Heeresgruppe 'Weichsel'* were now clear as day and quite simple:

1.) Carry on the breakthrough to the west to the Baltic coast and, in the heart of Germany, to Berlin toward the Western Powers.

2.) Roll up the Vistula Front by an early turn toward the north, roughly between Bromberg and Schneidemühl.

Now a third *Kessel*[4] would be added to the Kurland *Kessel* and the one nearly completed in East Prussia. There was a new and favorable opportunity to smash the entire German northern wing in separate parts. In light of their previous experience with *Feldherr* Hitler's command, the Russian command could count on the situation to develop in this manner with almost dead certainty. The previously described concentration of the Russian forces presented the opportunity to the Germans for an entirely possible formation of a *Schwerpunkt* [point of main concentration] on the German Northern Front, but only through the withdrawal of the Kurland forces that were no longer in the reckoning at all.

Marshal Zhukov knew his opponent's practice of dividing his forces all too well. Only on that basis is it possible to comprehend the boldness, one might almost say recklessness, of his further operations in the German eastern territory east of the Oder. Certainly the overall inferiority of the German forces with *Heeresgruppen 'Weichsel'* and *'Nord'* is beyond doubt. It can, nevertheless, be asserted that there was a viable possibility at that time for the German command to make this battle extremely difficult for the Russians. The road to Berlin would have been an arduous and costly struggle rather than an easy stroll.

In retrospect the question thereby arises whether the Western Powers would then have been forced to advance to the Oder and open the battle of Berlin from the west. That is a question that, despite Yalta, might possibly have had a by no means insignificant influence on the German eastern border, which was so hotly contested at that time.

How did the Commander-in-Chief of *Heeresgruppe 'Weichsel'*, Heinrich Himmler, evaluate the situation outlined above at that time? There is no knowing. He was simply not capable of a strategic evaluation of the big picture. He merely gazed, spellbound, at

---

4   Translator's note – literally 'kettle'. The usual English term is 'pocket'. I prefer to retain the German *Kessel* in situations like these because the dramatic scale is inadequately represented by the English term.

General der Infanterie Theodor Busse (centre), CO 9. *Armee*. This image was
taken in Russia, summer 1943. (Bundesarchiv 101I-219-0579A-21)

the immense gap that he had to close. He looked on the Russian advance south of the Netze towards Posen as a unique opportunity for him to strike the Russian flank from the Schneidemühl – Bromberg line, thereby to attack and smash them. He constantly used the word 'aggressively' and 'thrust into the flank.' It never occurred to him that the Russians were planning to attack the flank of his own, hard-struggling 2nd *Armee*. One look at the map that was always in front of him, however, would have made that obvious.

For him 'Attack' seemed the only alternative. He spoke seriously about the 2nd *Armee* renewing the attack as soon as the gap was sealed – idle dreaming. What forces were then available to the *Heerresgruppe* to use in an attack? In a word – the weak security forces between Bromberg and Schneidemühl and the garrisons of these two so-called fortresses. As I remember, there was a single weak division of hastily thrown-together fortress troops in Bromberg (the Thorn garrison, also about one weak division, was at that time encircled and only arrived in Bromberg days later). The 15th *lettische SS Freiwilligen-Division* [15th Latvian SS Volunteeer-Division] was committed as security on both sides of Nakel. The fortress garrison in Schneidemühl consisted of hastily thrown-together troops, in part *Volkssturm* with a strength of about eight battalions of infantry, a few pioneers and the fortress artillery.

According to *Führerbefehl* [special orders from the *Führer*] the fortress garrisons had to remain in their fortresses. With this force of troops, which, aside from the Latvians, were in no way capable of an orderly attack, Himmler wanted to launch a flank attack on about three to four Russian armies, including a tank army. There was no unified command of these troops, which were strung out along 80 kilometers. Above all, there was no secure communications link other than the postal network.[5]

Although this dealt with the southern flank of the 2nd *Armee*, Himmler himself wanted to direct this battle. He gave orders indiscriminately to individual battalions until it was possible to put a halt to that practice. I particularly remember that Himmler, who apparently did not know how to measure distances on a map and constantly confused the scales of the usual general staff maps, sent a battalion out from Schneidemühl, utterly alone, with the clear and simple mission of attacking the enemy (see strength above) and, initially, holding him until the flank attack took effect. At that point the battalion was to join in the attack. The battalion commander, an elderly reserve officer, was totally at a loss. He did not dare raise objections against his Commander-in-Chief. According to this assignment the battalion would end up in the open countryside 30 kilometers south of Schneidemühl with neither communications nor contact, because Himmler had no idea that ten centimeters on the map was about 30 kilometers on the ground. No more was ever heard of that battalion.

As a result of repeated urging, Himmler resolved to place the 'attack force' at the Netze river under unified command. My proposal was that the commander of the Latvian division be so designated. That was the simplest solution. His division was, more-or-less, the nucleus of the force. He had a division staff and some means of communications. Himmler, however, did not like that. There had to be a *Korps* staff. Fortunately it was possible to prevent the staff of the *stellvertretendes* [acting] *Generalkommando* II under its excellent commanding general, *General der Infanterie* Kienitz from receiving this

---

5 Translator's note – The civilian telephone system was operated by the postal service and was in no way secure from ordinary eavesdropping, let alone purposeful signals interception.

assignment regardless of the innumerable especially important tasks for which this staff had been committed here. By chance at this time *Obergruppenführer und General der Waffen-SS* Demmlhuber, nicknamed 'Tosca', (he generally smelled of this well-known perfume) was present. In Himmler's opinion, this was the right man for the job. A makeshift *Korps* staff of *Waffen-SS* was activated and, one day later, Demmlhuber sat in Nakel as Commanding General. He was not very inspired with this new mission.

After an adventurous retreat the staff of the 9th *Armee* finally arrived in Frankfurt-an-der-Oder. Its Commander-in-Chief was *General der Infanterie* Busse, its Chief of the General Staff, *Oberst i.G.* Hoelz. In *General* Busse I again met an old acquaintance and one-time direct superior. For a long time he was my *Ia* on the staff of *Feldmarschall* von Manstein, particularly during the fighting for Crimea and later at Stalingrad. Even at that time we anticipated a great career for this exceptionally gifted, clever and energetic general-staff officer. Now, barely two years later he was the Commander-in-Chief of an army.

It was a great help to me in the official relationships that became ever more difficult to be precisely known to this Commander-in-Chief, and, as would become evident, to have his entire confidence. Relationships with the 2nd *Armee* were similar. Here, however, the Chief of the General Staff, *Generalmajor* Macher, was an old acquaintance from difficult times in Russia. I would always be grateful to him, too, for a great trust in me that he was also able to pass on to his Commander-in-Chief.

Generalmajor Macher had been a *Korps* Chief of Staff with the 6th *Armee* during the period in 1943/44 when I was the First General-Staff Officer [*Ia*] there. We had worked particularly closely during the fighting retreat from the Dnjepr [Dnieper River] to Bessarabia.

The 9th *Armee* still had no combat-worthy troops. Aside from those in Fortress Posen the only troops attached to the 9th *Armee* at that time, the end of January, was V *SS Gebirgskorps* under *Obergruppenführer und General der Waffen-SS* Krüger. This so-called *Korps* actually consisted only of the *Korps* staff with hastily thrown-together alarm and *Volksturm* units in company and battalion strength. Its initial mission was to build a thin security line along the Warthe river on both sides of Posen without contact to north or south. So far as I remember, this *Korps* had for its mobile nucleus one *Sturmgeschütz Abteilung* [battalion]. Command relationships on this broad front were extremely difficult. There were no division staffs. The *Korps* commanded regiments and battalions, if it can be called that, over the postal [civilian public] telephone network. Thus there could be no serious talk of defense at the Warthe. The Russian attack on Posen put the above mentioned security forces to flight. Posen was encircled. A strong Russian assault force advanced astride the Warthe on Birnbaum, another west of Posen toward Bentschen. In order, above all, to firm up the situation for the 9th *Armee* in some way, defense of the Oder – Warthe position was ordered.

This position was an important element in the fortifications that had been prepared in peacetime for the German eastern border in the years before Hitler came to power. Although it was, indeed, no Maginot Line, nor a *Westwall*, it was, nevertheless, a very well constructed system of positions with all that pertained thereto. If it had been manned by an appropriate defensive force of combat-worthy troops in good time it would have provided a promising opportunity for a successful defensive battle, but only if the above prerequisites were met. If the troops were not on hand to properly man the position, then it would be no more and no less than the many other positions in the East, which, more or less well constructed, were generally only attained simultaneously with the pursuing enemy. Their defense was then mostly a matter of a few days.

Hitler and the *OKH* naturally placed great hopes in the Oder – Warthe position, as did Himmler. Here, in this nearly impregnable position the Russians must be brought to a halt.

Part III

By this time the intended Chief of the General Staff, *SS Brigadeführer und Generalmajor der Waffen-SS* Lammerding, had arrived at the *Heeresgruppe*. I had eagerly awaited his arrival, because the burden of work and responsibility threatened to overwhelm me. Based on my previous experience in numerous commands, I hoped for significant relief and support from the new Chief. It must be understood how unusual and arduous it was, right at the beginning, to work with a Commander-in-Chief who had practically none of the basic knowledge required for such a position. This was especially difficult because he was a man from the political camp.

Lammerding was somewhere in his late thirties, coming from the original officer corps of the *Waffen-SS*. He came from the West. There he had spent several months as Commander of the 2nd *SS Panzer Division 'Das Reich'*. He did not appear very happy about his new position. His qualifications for the position of Chief-of-General-Staff of a *Heeresgruppe* consisted essentially of the fact that he had spent some time as *Ia* of an *SS Division* and even as Chief-of-Staff of an *SS Korps*. Those were somewhat slim qualifications for his present important position as Chief-of-General-Staff of the *Heeresgruppe*.

This deficiency of experience – one can better say lack of knowledge – in the command of large formations, affected his entire performance with the *Heeresgruppe*. With him, there was always the impression of insecurity. That was compounded by the fact that he was a cautious man, inclined towards compromise. In his new position, at least, he avoided taking personal responsibility. As a troop commander he had, certainly, been a competent, courageous soldier. Initially he did not involve himself in the business of commanding the *Heeresgruppe* and let things, as one says, come to him. He was particularly reticent in expressing to Himmler his views on the operational situation. To Himmler[1] he was most optimistic. When alone, and internally, it is certain that he was always so. Therefore I did not get the hoped-for relief, rather, I had even more to do in order to brief the new Chief of the General-Staff on all that had taken place hitherto and that had already been planned.

Two days after Lammerding's arrival the *Heeresgruppe* staff – it must have been in the final days of January – moved from Deutsch-Krone to the Crössinsee *Ordensburg* near Falkenburg in Pomerania.[2] The reason for the move was the Russian advance on Schneidemühl and the attendant increasing threat to Deutsch-Krone.

---

1 Footnote in original document –This is probably a typographical error. It should probably read 'Hitler' instead of Himmler.

2 Translator's note - The term *Ordensburg* generally refers to 'order castles' built by the Teutonic knights in the Middle Ages. The Nazi Party later adopted the term for the newly-built structures housing the educational institutions that, it hoped, would educate the future leaders of party and country. The *Ordensburg* at Falkenburg in Pomerania was one of three *Ordensburg* (order-castles) constructed in the late 1930's to house and school physically perfect, immaculately Aryan candidates between 25 and 30 years of age, carefully selected from the Nazi Party, Hitler Youth, *SA* (Brownshirts, *Sturmabteilung*) or *SS* (*Schützstaffel*, Blackshirts). The outbreak of war in 1939 ended this program. The well-built stark stone structures were then used for other purposes.

SS Brigadeführer Heinz Lammerding (right), Chief of Staff *Heeresgruppe 'Weichsel'* 24 January-21 March 1945. A photograph taken in Russia, summer 1943. (Bundesarchiv 101I-219-0579A-01A)

It is obvious that a *Heeresgruppe-* or *Armee-* staff cannot operate immediately behind the front line. It can have an advanced command post for the Commander-in-Chief. The staff, however, has to be sufficiently removed from the front line so that it can work and not suddenly be forced to break off its labors by one of the numerous accidents of war. Such a staff requires a certain amount of time to set up, less for actual housing than, primarily, for its far-reaching, intricately branched communications network, without which it would be helpless. During the two final years in the East, however, a particular refinement of Hitler's strategy, which he also required of armies and *Heeresgruppen*, was that they remain as far forward as possible. One may believe that it was no lack of personal courage that led Commanders-in-Chief to repeatedly require that their command posts make timely moves, but that these moves were required so that they could effectively command.

What one requires from the Commander-in-Chief of an army is not that he use a *Panzerfaust* in the front line but that he command his troops. In exactly the same fashion, *Gefreiter* Müller is expected to man his machine-gun, but not command the army. Hitler gradually inverted this. For example, and there were innumerable such in the East, I, myself, experienced two particularly crass examples:

In January 1943 the Staff of *Heeresgruppe 'Don',* commanded by *Feldmarschall* von Manstein, which was in command of the Stalingrad area, remained so long in Nowo-Tscherkask that the first Russian tanks entered the city while the staff was still there. In October 1943, at the end of the fighting retreat from the Mius river to the Dnjepr river the command post of the 6th *Armee* remained four days in Bereslaw, separated from the enemy only by the width of a river. Only a few houses distant from them were the regimental- and battalion- staffs of the units in that sector. For the command of the army there were available two telephones in two little *panje-* rooms [typical peasant rooms] in which the Commander-in-Chief, Chief-of-Staff, *Ia* with about four to five *Ordonnanzoffizieren*, along with several clerks, draftsmen and communications men lived and worked. Berislaw was under Russian fire. At that time I was *Ia* of this staff. Even at the risk of being taken for a 'nervous-Nellie' I finally demanded that the command post be removed to a place where the staff could work and command. This was not because of the gunfire, but because of the need for space and, above all, because the lack of communications rendered command impossible. The only reason that we had remained there was that the Commander-in-Chief of the 6th *Armee* at that time, *Generaloberst* Hollidt, did not want it said that the army had moved its command post prematurely.

Such allegations continually came up. They often had a decidedly negative effect on command. In contrast it must be pointed out that the *Führerhauptquartier* was always located at secure places far from the front. That was entirely in order. One must merely permit the other higher organs of command the same latitude for reasons of due caution. As for the personal commitment of the German higher commanders of the army, the count of about 250 generals killed in action or who died as a result of their wounds is the best evidence. It is probable that the generals of the army thereby suffered, percentage-wise, the highest overall losses in killed and wounded in the war.[3]

The old front-soldier of the First World War, Hitler, however, held that it was unnecessary for him, as Supreme Commander to go even to the *Heeresgruppen* or *Armeen*, let alone to the front. I know of only three occasions during the Eastern Campaign when Hitler dared to leave his secure hole. One of these was a visit to *Feldmarschall* von Kluge at *Heeresgruppe 'Mitte'* in Smolensk in 1942. There was a visit to *Feldmarschall* von Manstein at *Heeresgruppe 'Süd'* in Shaporosha in 1944 and a visit to *Heeresgruppe 'Weichsel'* in March 1945. Regarding this last it must be realized that this final visit was not by Hitler's free choice but only under extreme pressure of the Commander-in-Chief who wanted, for once, to speak with his Supreme Commander outside of the atmosphere of the *Führerhauptquartier*. All rumours of a visit by Hitler in the *Kessel* of Demjansk or even Stalingrad, etc. were pure inventions of party propaganda. Here Hitler could have, above all, followed the example of Mr Churchill, whom he so often maligned.

That statesman and leader of England in the most difficult conflict of its history stands as a paragon of how a responsible head-of-state should show and, if necessary, commit his person in wartime, not only at the conference table but also in the theater of war. It is not known that Mr Churchill, who was also an officer and soldier, ever said anything about *'Frontsoldatentum'*.[4] On the other hand, he repeatedly and frequently made personal appearances both during the fighting in Africa and also during the invasion in the West, often in dangerous situations and where fighting was in progress.

One can read about these visits of Churchill to the front in the extremely interesting diary of the naval adjutant of General Eisenhower titled *My Three Years with Eisenhower*[5] and discover how significant these were to the military command. Churchill never

---

3 Translator's note - It is not entirely clear with whom the generals of the army [*Heer*] are being compared so far as their percentage killed or dead of wounds is concerned.

4 Translator's note -*'Frontsoldatentum'* is not very translatable. It is a term Hitler used to refer to a special mystique or ethos associated with the 'soldier who served at the front', a romanticized and extremely politicized concept arising from the First World War. While similar separations in viewpoint and understanding between the common soldier at the front and the rest of society arose in every nation involved in the war, this concept acquired special significance in the postwar politics of Germany, where the myth grew that the *Frontsoldat* had been 'stabbed in the back' by the politicians at home.

5 Butcher, Captain, USNR, Harry C., *My Three Years With Eisenhower – Naval Aid to General Eisenhower, 1942 – 1945*, Simon & Schuster, 1946.

attempted to play '*Feldherr*'[6] He had, however, taken his full share of the responsibility for the direction and command of the war on the spot and, as it appears to me, given extremely practical advice. And this says nothing regarding the additional mobility that this remarkable man evidenced during the war with his numerous great flights to America, Moscow and the like, which were, certainly, not without danger.

At the Krössinsee *Ordensburg* I learned, for the first time, as a soldier and, indeed, under the special circumstances of the war, of one of the seminaries for the nurture of the future leading men of the party and state. Much had been heard of them, especially because it was from these *Ordensburgen* that the schooling of *General* Schörner's *NSFO* (*Nationalsozialisticher Führungsoffizier*) originated.[7]

We could no longer form a real picture of the life and activity of such an *Ordensburg* since its last sucklings, the so-called *Ordensjunker*, had long since departed. Thus we could only gain an impression of the externals.

The first impression of the Krössinsee *Ordensburg* was of a military camp like the training grounds so familiar to a soldier. There were long, regular rows of brick dormitories with large flat green lawns and simple gardens. The arrangement of these brick dormitories which had served the *Ordensjunkers* for quarters and work places was simple and reminiscent of military barracks. They had, however, a certain style, a somewhat studied and, therefore, not genuine, Nordic style dominated by natural wood and forged iron as the basic elements. As best I remember there was also a great deal of colorful runic painting. Particularly conspicuous were the extremely massive, long, narrow, scrubbed white wooden tables of the dining hall with rather uncomfortable chairs in matching style. The common dining hall was immense, a mixture of Germanic hall and cathedral. Tremendously high-ceilinged, this room took up an entire building. All in all, everything was set up for mass-handling and, so far as it concerned the premises of the *Ordensjunker*, extremely simple.

The actual '*Burg*' was in contrast to the above. It was a large castle-like brick building. At one time it served as residence for the '*Burgvogt*', as the leader of the *Ordensburg* was called. Presumably the teachers and instructors at that time also lived there. A large number of the rooms, however, were set aside for the planned dwelling of the *Reichsorganisationsleiter* Dr. Ley, with corresponding prestigious rooms and guest quarters. This castle was, in truth, luxuriously furnished in all its elements, especially in the quarters alluded to and the lounges, but in no sense tasteful. There was no such thing as a consistent style. The overall effect was rather ostentatious, if not to say *nouveau-riche*, even though the individual pieces of furniture were certainly costly and many

---

6   Translator's note - Here, again, is a term that has special significance in German history for which there is no English term that quite includes all the associations. Frederick the Great, who was Hitler's idol, is the exemplar of all that *Feldherr* represents: The great field-commander who was, at once, the national leader and the brilliant general controlling all the events on the battlefield, the strategic genius under whose personal command great events unfolded. The traditional picture is of the *Feldherr* directing the battle from a conveniently placed little hill with a commanding view of the battlefield.

7   Translator's note - Toward the end of the war, *NSFO* were assigned to field units of the army to see to the correct party indoctrination and beliefs of the army soldiers and officers.

actually beautiful. Here, however, German workshop furniture and handcrafts were mixed indiscriminately with genuine old pictures, furniture and carpets.[8]

Himmler established his headquarters, for the time being, in this *Ordensburg.* It would have been more accurate, so far as his person went, to have called it his residence.

The situation on the *Heeresgruppe* front worsened daily. At this point it was marked by the following events:

In the 9th *Armee* sector Posen was finally encircled. The battle for the fortress had begun. Robbed of its central feature, the weak security forces on both sides of Posen – V *SS Gebirgskorps* – had been forced back everywhere and were now retreating to the Oder – Warthe position. The enemy advanced unopposed toward Küstrin. The Russians had already built several small bridgeheads on the north shore in the face of the weak flank-security along the Netze. There was fighting around Bromberg. The main body of the 2nd *Armee* had fallen back to the Vistula. It still held bridgeheads at Kulm, Graudenz and Marienwerder. The northern wing of the army still stood in firm contact east of the river, directly east of the line Marienwerder – Marienburg – Elbing.

The enemy's primary offensive intentions were already clear, even though he actually attacked everywhere on a broad front.

One group of forces, south of the Warthe, was advancing with its main direction of advance via Frankfurt-an-der-Oder along the shortest route to Berlin. Since Posen was a decisive transportation hub on this route, the enemy was forced to capture this city with all the forces that were so abundantly available to him. Here the Russians acted very differently than at Thorn. The strength of this southern group consisted of about one tank army and two to three regular armies. An additional group of forces of one tank army and two to three armies, between the Warthe and Netze rivers with its leading elements already north of the Netze was advancing toward Küstrin and the lower Oder between Küstrin and Stettin, with its final objective also Berlin. A third group of forces attacked the entire width of the front of the 2nd *Armee* with the apparent objective of forcing simultaneous crossings over the Weichsel in as many places as possible in order to build a defensive strongpoint and, at the same time, to prevent withdrawal of German forces for use elsewhere.

Continuous attacks across the Netze river toward the north in increasing strength made clear the enemy's actual intention. Whether or not the frontal attack over the Vistula was successful or not, a thrust into the deep flank was building there, which, in the event that it did not break through, could, in any case, be transformed into an envelopment of the 2nd *Armee* in the general direction of the Baltic coast west of Danzig. The Russian forces facing the 2nd *Armee* were estimated at three to four armies supported by one tank army. Where, now, was the Russian *Schwerpunkt*? That was a vital question when considering countermeasures. At the time of the enemy situation described above, there was still no clear enemy *Schwerpunkt*. So far as strength was concerned, the three enemy forces were roughly equal. One could, however, consider the possibility of two *Schwerpunkte. Schwerpunkt* 1: A thrust to Berlin. *Schwerpunkt* 2 would be against the 2nd *Armee*, probably by the southern flank group of forces.

---

8   Translator's note - Rolf Sawinski's *Die Ordensburg Krössinsee in Pommern. Ein Bildband zur Geschichte der Ordensburg 'Die Falkenburg am Krössinsee'* (Euskirchen, privately published, 1997) presents the history of the Krössinsee *Ordensburg* and, briefly, of its sister institutions with extensive photographs, many from the early days, showing the unusual architecture and facilities.

Both Himmler and the Chief-of-the-General Staff considered this evaluation of the enemy situation, which I presented at that time, as too far-reaching and too pessimistic. They considered talk of a drive to Berlin to be an exaggeration. The threat to the 2nd *Armee* was not taken seriously. However, there was no more talk of a German flank attack over the Netze river to destroy the Russians. At that time Himmler concerned himself with only three points in the *Heeresgruppe* situation - the battle for the three fortresses of Posen, Schneidemühl and Thorn. It appeared that, in his opinion, the fate of the *Heeresgruppe* depended on the fate of these three fortresses. Actually only Posen influenced the bigger situation, because it nearly blocked the necessary Russian supply route. If, however, one remembers what was said above regarding the strength and defensive capabilities of these three fortresses, these battles could only be episodes without lasting effect. Above everything, Himmler could not provide any assistance in these fortress-battles. To be sure, he continually sent radio messages of both inspiration and blame. These, however, no longer had any positive effect. The fate of Thorn has already been reported. Posen and, especially, Schneidemühl put up truly heroic defenses against overwhelmingly superior enemy forces. When the fates of these two cities were already sealed, meaning when the only foreseeable outcome was the purposeless massacre of the remnants of the garrisons, the Chief of the General Staff tried again and again to get the breakout orders sought by the commandants of the fortresses from Himmler. It was impossible. The unfortunate order of Hitler's, 'Where the German soldier once makes his stand, he does not give way', also sputtered in the head of his faithful servant. In addition, Himmler, in his insecurity as a military leader, simply lived in constant fear of the displeasure of his lord and master.

This anxiety about Hitler completely dominated the feared *Reichsführer-SS*. It made him incapable of energetically presenting any conception of the military situation to Hitler, let alone persuading him to accept it. This servile attitude caused much damage and cost a great deal of unnecessary blood.

At both Posen and Schneidemühl it would have been possible, as the courageous fortress commanders desired, to break out and, thereby, save at least the last of the combatants for other missions, of which the *Heeresgruppe* certainly had enough. The remnants of the garrison of Posen would have been a vital reinforcement to the Oder – Warthe position. The Schneidemühl garrison would have made it possible to delay the rapid Russian breakthrough to Küstrin by enabling some preparation for the defense of that important corner-post of the Oder defense. When it was too late, Hitler approved the breakout from the two fortresses. Only a few stragglers from Posen were able to report on the fall of the last German troops that had been forced back into the close confines of the so-called 'nucleus' [*Kernwerk*]. The *Kommandant* of Schneidemühl, *Oberstleutnant* Remlinger managed to break out with the sorry survivors of his troops. His fate, too, was sealed on what had, in the meantime, become too long a path through the enemy to the German front.

We have now gotten a bit ahead of the course of events. The *Heeresgruppe* stayed only a few days – four to five days, as I remember – in Krössinsee. Then came another hasty change of position to Hassleben near Prenzlau. The move came as a result of the fall of Schneidemühl. One could, however, deduce far more from this change of position. For a *Heeresgruppe* which had to command a front extending from Crossin on the Oder to Elbing in East Prussia, Prenzlau was entirely in the wrong position. This placed the headquarters behind the left wing of the front in Brandenburg when the fighting was to be in West Prussia and Pomerania. The proper place would actually have been Kolberg. It has already been emphasized how insistent Hitler was that headquarters of higher staffs were to be as far forward as possible. Here, however, there was an entirely different solution. One is forced to consider that the German supreme command was not as serious about the defense of West Prussia and Pomerania as it professed to be. Was it, perhaps, that *OKH* secretly doubted the possibility of maintaining the continuity of the over-stretched *Heeresgruppe 'Weichsel'* front? In fact, the continuity of that front had never even been established. If there were such doubts, then the *Schwerpunkt* of the *Heeresgruppe* would be on the Oder to defend Berlin. In that case, Prenzlau was in the right place for the command post. But how, then, should the 2nd *Armee* be commanded? This question was already urgent for the *Heeresgruppe* command. That forced decisive conclusions, especially regarding the fate of the German eastern provinces, their population and the major troop formations fighting there.

Since, in a forest camp near Hassleben the requisite communications links were not yet established at the time of the change of position, especially for command of the 2nd *Armee* and the fragmented units in Eastern Pomerania, a small command staff was initially left behind at Krössinsee. It was to follow along to Hassleben as soon as communications were set up. According to statements by *Generalmajor* Melzer, the communications commander of the *Heeresgruppe*, that would take two to three days. Such things happen in war, particularly when the situation is in a state of flux, even though they should be avoided whenever possible. The communications commander of any higher staff has to learn, as soon as possible, the location of its next position so that he can have his comprehensive work completed when the staff arrives. That is the only way that the requisite continuity of command can be assured. When the situation requires establishment of an advanced command post, as in this case, the basic rule is that either the Commander-in-Chief with his *Ia* [operations officer] or the Chief of the General Staff with another general staff officer remain at the old command post. Generally the Commander-in-Chief remains there as the responsible commander while the Chief of the General Staff prepares the new command post. Himmler did otherwise. He and his Chief of the General Staff proceeded to Hassleben and left the *Ia* and a few *Ordonnanzoffizieren* [special duty staff officers] behind.

If the situation had been calm and normal, that could have been accepted as an exception. In the situation at hand, however, it was to be expected that, particularly respecting the 2nd *Armee* and the battle in East Pomerania, vital decisions would be required on a nearly hourly basis. Such decisions could only be made by the Commander-in-Chief. That placed me, as *Ia*, in a truly difficult situation. It is only thanks to the trust, the understanding and the great sense of responsibility of the command of the 2nd *Armee*, especially its Commander-in-Chief, *Generaloberst* Weiß, that a further, appropriate exercise of command, also from the viewpoint of the *Heeresgruppe*, was, for the most part, possible. These days were extremely difficult for the few remaining officers and myself, since, for this short period, a substantial part of the responsibility rested entirely upon us.

Part IV

In the organization of the *Heeresgruppe* it was clear from the very beginning that it was lacking an *Armee* staff to take command at the endangered location, namely in the center, at that time approximately at the border, north of the Netze. It would have been simplest to pull one of the superfluous, fully functional *Armee* staffs out of the East Prussia – Kurland area and attach it to the *Heeresgruppe*. That, however, Hitler did not allow in his obsession to delude even himself by having the largest possible number of *Armee* flags on his situation map.

Thus a new *Armee* staff was activated by the *Waffen-SS* and the 11th *SS Panzer-Armee* was born. Himmler had learned nothing from the activation of his own staff. Again he saw an opportunity to engage in dynastic politics for the *Waffen-SS*. Hitherto he had striven to have the highest possible number of *Waffen-SS Korps* staffs. Now he had to have an *SS Armee*. It was not entirely clear why it was to be a *Panzerarmee*, since, at that point we had only three *Panzer* divisions in the *Heeresgruppe*. Apparently, however, *Panzerarmee* sounded better. Again, it was an amateurish game in the most serious of situations. More will be said about the success that Himmler had with his higher *SS* staffs.

The Commander-in-Chief of the new 11th *SS Panzerarmee* was *Obergruppenführer und General der Waffen-SS* Felix Steiner, formerly Commanding General of the III *SS Panzerkorps*. His Chief of General Staff was *Oberst i.G.* Estor, an army general staff officer. I knew them both, the latter particularly well from the difficult time in Rumania in 1944 where he had been my neighbour and colleague as *Ia* of the 8th *Armee*. In *Obergruppenführer* Steiner Himmlar had, undoubtedly, chosen the best available candidate from the officer corps of the *Waffen-SS*. Steiner was an experienced soldier who had proven himself in command of regiments, divisions and as Commanding General [*Korps*]. He had been an active [regular army, *Heeres*] officer in the First World War. He was, personally, particularly fresh and flexible and, along with *Oberstgruppenführer* Hauser, was probably the only other higher officer of the *Waffen-SS* who possessed the qualifications for high military command.

The advance party of this new *Armee* staff arrived in Krössinsee one day after Himmler's departure and was to establish its headquarters there. The *Heeresgruppe* was not yet able to decide what sector this 11th *SS Panzerarmee* was to receive. The organization and command relationships at the inner wings of the 9th and 2nd *Armeen* were, at that time, extremely unclear. Only after clarification of this relationship could the 11th *SS Panzerarmee* be inserted. During the night following Himmler's departure from Krössinsee I had a conversation with the Chief of the General Staff of the 2nd *Armee* in which, once more, he emphatically expressed to me his serious concerns for the south flank of his *Armee* and its contact with the 9th *Armee*. *Generaloberst* Weiß joined the conversation, expressing the same concern. This stimulated me to make a new evaluation of the overall situation of *Heeresgruppe* 'Weichsel'.

I perceived the entire magnitude of the danger, not only for the *Heeresgruppe*, but for the entire northern portion of the Eastern Front, and also the immense significance of

Obergruppenführer und General der Waffen-SS Felix Steiner, shown during an award ceremony in late 1942. Steiner was CO 11. *SS-Panzerarmee,* and later commanded the *ad-hoc* formation *Armeegruppe 'Steiner'.* (Bundesarchiv 101III-Moebius-139-08)

our situation in the further battle for what was left of Germany. Accordingly I decided to immediately send this necessarily extremely serious evaluation to Himmler by teletype. I was driven to this resolve as by an inner compulsion. My evaluation concluded that the Supreme German Command must immediately decide whether it would evacuate Kurland and East Prussia in order to hold West Prussia, Pomerania, the Grenzmark and Silesia, to the extent that these were still in our hands, or whether they would continue to allow the Russian breakthrough through the center of the *Heeresgruppe* 'Weichsel' front that was directly imminent. In that case the 2nd *Armee* would be cut off and destroyed in West Prussia, Pomerania would be lost and, after these losses, there would no longer be sufficient forces available to defend the Oder. The effects of such a development of the situation on the entire further German conduct of the war was obvious. In light of this great responsibility of the Commander-in-Chief of *Heeresgruppe* 'Weichsel' I asked Himmler, without consideration of any other misgivings, personally and immediately to go to Hitler. He must present this to Hitler with total clarity and demand a correspondingly immediate decision for the further conduct of the war on the northern portion of the German Eastern Front. The teletype with this evaluation of the situation, filling about three pages of teletype, was transmitted during the night to the new command post. Its receipt and delivery were acknowledged in the morning.

Based on my previous experience with Himmler I held no great hopes for any effect. I believed, however, that I had done my duty. Considering Himmler's attitude, this might well have serious consequences for me. In general, there was no comprehension of or tolerance for such unvarnished truth which would, in the last analysis, be seen as criticism of Hitler. The unwelcome bearer of such truths often vanished without a trace.

I never received an answer to this evaluation. Two days later I also hastened to the new command post, which was, by then, fully usable. I was, of course, in suspense about what the Commander-in-Chief and the Chief of the General Staff would say about my analysis of the situation. Initially they said nothing at all. They muddled onward as usual. Finally I asked Grothmann, Himmler's Chief Adjutant, whether or not the teletype had arrived. He told me that he had passed it on to the Chief of the General Staff who, in turn, would decide according to the importance of the contents, whether and when it would be presented to Himmler.

So it depended on *Brigadeführer* Lammerding. He explained to me that there was no way he could present such a document to Himmler. There was certainly a great deal of truth in that. In the existing situation Himmler would only have misunderstood that analysis. The only outcome would have been trouble for me and subsequent loss of Himmler's confidence. Himmler would never present anything like that to the *Führer*, let alone urge it on him. Himmler, however, must have learned something about it in the meantime. When I attempted to present this analysis of the situation to him personally, he refused to read it since it was –by now, indeed, four days old – outdated and we had, at the moment, more urgent concerns. I then brought the evaluation to the attention of the other general staff officers of the command section and it was entered in the *Armee* war diary with appropriate annotation. As was so often the case in this war, important documents of this sort found their way, unutilized, into the war diaries.

Upon my arrival at the new headquarters I found it was still in a state of confusion. People were still getting things arranged. In addition a general staff officer of the *Operationsabteilung* [operations section of *OKH*] *Oberstleutnant i.G. Freiherr* von

Humboldt was waiting for me. He came on an assignment from the Chief of the General Staff, *Generaloberst* Guderian, to be briefed on the situation. Apparently *OKH* had received little information during the time of my absence, particularly regarding the situation of the 2nd *Armee*. *Oberstleutnant* von Humboldt, who worked in the *Operationsabteilung* of *Heeresgruppe 'Weichsel'*[1] passed on to me serious objections, in the name of his Chief, regarding the lack of precision in reports, delayed arrival of situation maps and daily reports and more of the same. My explanations about the condition of the so-called *Heeresgruppe* staff with which we were forced to work in such a serious situation accomplished little with the young man. Either he did not believe me or considered that these were laughable excuses. Certainly it would have been hard for a man from *OKH* with its nearly unique technical command facilities to believe that a newly activated staff would still have week-long difficulties and friction. I finally categorically demanded help from *OKH* with regard to matériel and additional workers for the staff. They were promised but nothing came of it.

Accordingly the covert and open aspersions about the inadequate work of the *Heeresgruppe* in comparison with other higher staffs continued, until it would result in an emphatic clarification of these questions. More on that later. I was already familiar with this sort of badgering – I can call it by no other name – which was *OKH* practice in dealing with subordinate commands from my time as *Ic* [staff intelligence officer] with *Heeresgruppe 'Don'*.

It arose from the dreadful anxiety of the *Operationsabteilung* about the so-called *'Führerlage'* [the daily briefing of the *Führer* on the military situation]. Obviously, the Chief of the General Staff had to have the requisite documents for the daily situation briefing with Hitler. That was also clear to us lowly general staff officers outside of *OKH*. Since, however, the *'Führerlage'* started at 1500 hours, one could only require a situation report as of about 1000 hours in the morning and, even that, only if functioning communications existed, at least to the *Korps* level. *Generaloberst* Guderian was known to be rather rough. His situation, at this point, as Chief of the General Staff of the *Heer* [*Heer* refers to 'The Army' as a whole. *Armee* refers to 'an army', such as the 2nd *Armee* or the 9th *Armee*] was by-no-means enviable. He, too, was under intense pressure regarding the *'Führerlage'*. Thus it is entirely understandable on a human level that he drove the Chief of the *Operationsabteilung* and his young men all the more when the situation became even more unclear and difficult. But even that had to have limits, particularly with *Heeresgruppe 'Weichsel'* with its unique command situation. The *Operationsabteilung* understood no such boundaries. It was laughable to explain to trained general staff officers how long it took for a message to travel from the front line to the *Heeresgruppe* staff when there were no problems along the way. They had, indeed, learned that at the *Kriegsakademie*. These obvious things, however, were no longer seen when they were under pressure from their General Staff Chief, who was, likewise, under pressure. The *Führer* demanded it, so the *Heeresgruppe* and, in this case, always, the *Ia* had to provide it. It must be made clear that I, as *Ia*, never demanded that the 6th *Armee* require impossible

---

1   Translator's note – Despite the previous statement that he worked in the *Operationsabteilung* of *Heeresgruppe 'Weichsel'*, apparently a typographical error, *Oberstleutnant i.G.* von Humboldt appears to have worked in the *Operationsabteilung* of *OKH* and to have been sent from *OKH* by Guderian on this mission.

situation reports from its attached *Korps*, even though the superior *Heeresgruppe* at that time demanded much that was impossible in that area. This perpetual pressure from above, this total inability to accept delay, doubtless resulted in too many imprecise, if not downright incorrect, reports. Gradually the basic rule developed that it was better to give a report that was not entirely clear than no report at all, simply to avoid this ceaseless slave-driving from above. The end result was that even a general staff officer had to keep his eyes and ears as much on the superior command to the rear as on the situation at the front. I often said to my colleagues and also to Himmler that the war with *OKH* was more difficult and exhausting than that with the Russians. Thus the relationship between *OKH* and *Heeresgruppe 'Weichsel'* grew ever more strained.

The new headquarters of the *Heeresgruppe* – a forest camp between Prenzlau and Hassleben – had actually been set up as an alternative location to avoid the bombing for the offices of the *Reichsführer-SS*. It was an extensive barrack-camp with, I would estimate, about 20 large *RAD* barracks [*Reichsarbeitsdienst, Reich* Labor Service] disposed in the woods on both sides of the Hassleben – Prenzlau road, surrounded by a high wire fence. Although situated in the forest, it was poorly camouflaged from aerial observation. While most of the barracks were rather simply set up for housing and work areas, the so-called *'Reichsführer* barrack' was an exception. It was substantially larger and specially constructed. Its interior facilities corresponded to its exalted function. Himmler's quarters were at its south end, consisting of an extremely large work-room, painted in bright colors with costly furniture. The bedroom was exceedingly elegant, in reddish wood. With its eiderdown quilts, furnishings and carpets in light green it was more a bedroom for a great lady than for a man who commanded troops in war. There was also a sort of dining room for private dining with a select few. The remaining assigned quarters in this 'barrack' corresponded to its high function, housing only Himmler's closest co-workers, such as his Chief Adjutant, Chief of the Ministerial Chancellory and a few aids and female secretaries. The other rooms were also quite elegantly furnished. There were large lounges and dining rooms, several baths and the necessary housekeeping areas. The main entry of this building in the center of the long front-facade led into a sort of vestibule remarkable for several Göbelin-style hand-woven tapestries decorating the walls. They came from *SS* workshops, had Nordic colors and were quite tasteless. The solidly made and tasteful furniture likewise came from the workshops of the *SS*, the beautiful porcelains from the *SS* porcelain factory. It was something new to me that there were such things, even in the midst of total war. Only Himmler's closest personal staff was quartered in this *'Reichsführer* barrack.' As for the staff of the *Heeresgruppe*, only Lammerding, the Chief of the General Staff resided there. The actual *Heeresgruppe* staff, that is, the command section [*Führungsabteilung*], was in the other barracks. The logistics section [*Oberquartiermeisterabteilung*] and all the others were housed in Prenzlau.

To conclude these externals, which only add a bit of colour to the picture, I shall sketch a day of work with Himmler. It must be emphasized that the 'affairs of the court' [*'höfische Teil'*], as we called it at the time, will be particularly described. It took up a major part of the Commander-in-Chief's time. Generally, it had nothing to do with the work of the *Heeresgruppe*.

Himmler was accustomed to arise relatively late, at about 0830 hours. After his bath he then went to his masseur. This somewhat bloated and disagreeable individual played a considerable role with Himmler and had, it was said, not-insignificant influence. Generally Himmler's personal physician, *Prof. Dr.* Gebhardt also came to the 'levée'. He would, shortly, be condemned to death in a medical trial at Nürnberg. *Prof. Dr.* Gebhardt, well-known Chief Physician at Höhenlychen, *SS Truppenführer und Generalleutnant der Waffen-SS* was, at that time, also *Heeresgruppenarzt*, that is, the responsible director of the military medical activity of the *Heeresgruppe*. *Prof.* Gebhardt was probably one of Himmler's closest intimates.[2]

Prof. Dr. Gebhardt's influence seemed to me to be particularly great. He had access to Himmler at any hour and was often present as a listener at purely military matters relating to the command of the *Heeresgruppe*. As a result of his activity as personal physician to Himmler, Chief Physician at Hohenlychen, and the fact that he was also president of the German Red Cross, he had little time to be concerned with his duties as *Heeresgruppe* surgeon. These duties were, essentially, taken care of by *Oberstarzt Prof. Dr.* Eimer, a particularly energetic and gifted medical officer and physician.

Himmler generally breakfasted at about 1000 hours. He started his official day at 1030 hours. First came the situation briefing by the Chief of Staff, *Ia* [operations] and, usually, also the *Ic* [intelligence]. That generally took from half an hour to an hour. If time remained before lunch, then came the gentlemen of the *'Feldkommandostelle Reichsführer-SS* [Himmler's field-command post for his many responsibilities *other than* commanding the *Heeresgruppe*]. First came Chief Adjutant Grothmann and Ministerial Director Brandt, who was also condemned to death in the Nürnberg medical trials. Brandt was a calm, relatively modest man, an absolutely typical bureaucrat. It is incomprehensible that this man could be condemned to death as a war criminal. His primary talent, as I was told, was his stenography. He was one of the best stenographers in Germany and, as such, Himmler gradually promoted him from personal secretary to chief of his chancellery and ministerial director.

Frequently more or less high personages also came in the morning, generally higher *SS Führer* whom Himmler had summoned. Frequently Kaltenbrunner, the Chief of the *Gestapo* was among them. He also impressed me, in the brief opportunities I had to meet him, as a bureaucrat rather than as a bloodthirsty police chief. *Reichsmarschall* Hermann Göring was also a frequent visitor. More will be said later regarding these visits. Himmler dined punctually at 1300 hours, generally with the officers and officials of the *Feldkommandostelle*, the female secretaries and various guests. Himmler's standard of living with regard to food and drink was simple. The menu was south-German plain-cooking. At least once a week there was stew and once a week horse-meat. There was wine only when guests were present. Otherwise fruit juice was the beverage. Himmler ate very quickly, smoked a cigar and then took a midday nap. At about 1500 hours he was again available. That was when reports were presented. Supper was served at 1900 hours, equally simple. Here, too, Himmler withdrew very quickly, for then came the evening presentation by the Chief of the General Staff and *Ia*. During these sessions

---

2   Translator's note – Hohenlychen, a well-known sanatorium and health resort since its founding by the Berlin Red Cross in 1902, came into disrepute in the late 1930's under *Dr.* Gebhardt. In the Nürnberg trials he and his deputies were accused of brutal 'medical experimentation' upon concentration camp inmates there and at the nearby Ravensbruck concentration camp. Gebhardt was sentenced to death, and was hanged on 2 June 1948.

he generally summoned the Commanders-in-Chief of the *Armeen* to give him a final picture of the situation. Occasionally he then concluded by talking with the Chief of the General Staff of the *Heer*, *Generaloberst* Guderian and telling him about the latest events. It was, more accurately, narration rather than serious discussion of the ever-worsening situation.

Apparently Himmler had once heard somewhere that a Commander-in-Chief was supposed to conduct such evening discussions, and therefore he did the same. *Generaloberst* Guderian often requested that these discussions finally come to an end. Whenever possible, Himmler retired to bed at 2230 hours. He did not like to be disturbed after that. He gave the impression that he was neither physically nor psychologically very robust. After 2300 hours he was usually so tired that he could no longer follow any sort of reports.

It is quite usual, however, in difficult situations, that the Commander-in-Chief has to work right through until morning and must often be importuned. Himmler simply did not see such things through. It was quite unpleasant when he returned from the '*Führerlage*', which he frequently drove to Berlin for. Then he was so exhausted that it was hardly possible to discuss anything important with him. His lack of endurance was extremely burdensome and difficult for those who had to work with him. He generally did not allow his sleep to be disturbed.

Any Commander-in-Chief in wartime should be left undisturbed at night whenever possible. His colleagues do their best to spare him, but frequently he is required for urgent decisions. If that happened with Himmler, he was extremely discourteous and so sleepy that it was difficult to make things clear to him. This happened to me repeatedly. This was particularly disrupting for the command of the *Heeresgruppe*. Especially disturbing, however, were the numerous additional concerns that Himmler still had. He was, at the same time *Reichsminister des Innern* [interior minister], Chief of Police, *Reichsführer-SS* and Commander-in-Chief of the Replacement Army [*Oberbefehlshaber des Ersatzheeres*], all of which, at least marginally, played a significant role. Since, for some time, Himmler had also awarded, for Hitler, the high military decorations such as *Ritterkreuze* [Knight's Crosses] and *goldene Nahkampfspangen* [golden close-combat clasps], among others, that, too, took up considerable time. Once I was present at such a ceremony. It probably was a matter of concern to most of those present that, strangely enough, a man who was no soldier in any way was awarding these decorations with resounding words about courage and heroism.

Part V

After this special account we turn again to military events involving the *Heeresgruppe*. In the 9th *Armee* sector the remnants of V *Gebirgskorps*, comprising the *Korps* staff and remnants of a few alarm units, arrived in the Oder – Warthe position at the same time as the hard-pressing Russians. These minimal forces could only provide a trivial supplement to the only too-weakly manned position. The forces manning the position could best be described as a security garrison consisting of two division staffs with two to three battalions each of alarm and training units, inadequate artillery and as good as no defense against armour. Command within both of these divisions was extraordinarily difficult due to lack of sufficient communications equipment. The individual formations had only just been activated and knew nothing about each other, so there could be no talk about any kind of strong cohesion. There was nothing that the Commanding General of V *SS Gebirgskorps* could do about this. He had barely escaped being pocketed by the Russians as the attack on his new position started with full force. It is no longer possible to determine the details of this fighting at the Oder – Warthe position.

All that can be said of the position, upon which *OKH* had placed so many hopes, was that it was already breached at several locations on the first day. That was hardly any great surprise to any down-to-earth soldier considering the circumstances outlined above. Himmler, far more so Hitler and *OKH* raged. There was a feverish search for a scapegoat. The words 'court martial' and 'drumhead court martial' dominated this tragic situation. Above all, the two unfortunate division commanders, both generals of the *Heer*, were now to be called to account. The one was a *General* Vogt, who later proved himself most honorably at Arnswalde. I no longer remember the name of the other. Himmler spoke only of the incompetent and cowardly generals whom he planned to prosecute. Rather than do anything to help these men or, above all else, putting this not-unimportant sector of the front in some kind of order, there was nothing but a lot of commotion and complaint. The *Heeresgruppe* and, obviously, also its Commander-in-Chief, Himmler, shared at least equal accountability for the loss of this position. They had not provided in timely fashion for the urgently needed reinforcements. Himmler, himself, was by no means excused before his troops by the fact that his lord and master had made nothing available to him. Lacking here, even in the most critical locations, were the troops fighting in lost causes in Kurland and the remnants of East Prussia. In the event, the generals were not condemned to death, as intended. Instead, one was sent home and the other immediately employed elsewhere. Himmler removed the Commanding General of the V *SS Gebirgskorps*, *SS Obergruppenführer* Krüger, who could not really have done anything to prevent this misfortune and who had twice been cut off by the Russians and arduously broken out. He was, after Demlhuber, the second high *SS* commander who had displeased his lord. More would follow.

With the loss of the Oder – Warthe position the front of the 9th *Armee* fell back entirely to the Oder. Thereby all contact required for a defensive battle was lost between the central and northern *Armeen* of the *Heeresgruppe* (11th *SS Panzer-* and 2nd *Armee*).

Landsberg fell without significant opposition, since nothing was there. Himmler had sent a *Tiger-Abteilung* [battalion] of the *Waffen-SS* there all alone on the railroad. None of the protests of the *Führungsabteilung* [command section of the *Heeresgruppe* staff] against this impossible maneuver of the Commander-in-Chief did any good. Himmler actually believed that one *SS Tiger-Abteilung* could shatter a Russian tank army. The *Abteilung* was attacked by the Russians while it was still on the railroad train in Landsberg. Naturally, it could not detrain. With loss of three or four tanks that were still securely tied down on the rail-cars it returned after a narrow escape to Küstrin. Here, too, the commander of the *Panzerabteilung* was to be a whipping-boy. It was possible, however, to convince Himmler that a *Tiger* tank on a railroad car was severely handicapped when it came to fighting and that it was technically impossible for these proud steel predators, weighing about fifty tons, to simply leap down. The way to Küstrin, that historical old Prussian fortress, was now open to the Russians. From Küstrin to Berlin was only about eighty kilometers!

North of the Warthe and Netze, at the same time, the spearheads of the enemy attack had reached the general line Berlinchen – Arnswalde – Kallis – Deutsche Krone – Flatow (30 January 1945). Here the *Heeresgruppe* attempted to find a new front with the 11th *SS Panzerarmee*. The situation of this *Armee* was like that of a man who slips and falls into a shaft, and now seeks to halt his fall by trying to get a hold on the opposing walls with his arms and legs. Unfortunately, the shaft here was too wide. No matter how much reckoning and stretching, there was just no way to reach the walls on opposite sides. For the 11th SS *Panzerarmee* the two walls were the Oder river and the south wing of the 2nd *Armee* in the Tucheler *Heide*.

Thus, instead of a defensible front it was only possible to build a thin security line that, simply from pure considerations of terrain, had an unfavorable course. Only its right wing rested on weak natural obstacles. Nowhere did it have even makeshift prepared positions, nor did it have any sort of depth. It was predictable that the enemy would break though anywhere that he made a vigorous effort. It was impossible to form any sort of defensive strongpoints because of the lack of adequate forces.

In the meantime, the 2nd *Armee* had lost the Netze line with the fortress of Bromberg and been forced back to the north into the Tuchelor *Heide* in heavy, costly fighting. The Russians attacked on their Vistula front with undiminished force. The Kulm, Graudenz, Marienburg and Elbing bridgeheads were under extreme pressure. The loss of Kulm was imminent. This sort of bridgehead was similar to the fortresses, another of Hitler's *idée fixe*. Conventionally one only holds a bridgehead if one intends to launch a new operation from it and, above everything, if that operation is feasible. Here that was by no means possible. In this case these salients in the front – with the river to their rear – merely resulted in ongoing and useless expenditure of forces on a front that needed any forces that could possibly be freed up to be thrown into its seriously endangered southern flank.

The result was that the relatively strongest *Armee* of the *Heeresgruppe* with the substantial obstacle, the Vistula River, supporting its front, was gradually being bled dry by these bridgeheads that Hitler ordered to be held. The *Armee* had to look on while its southern flank was steadily forced back and see how, in the immediate future, it would lose the already loose contact with the 11th *SS Panzerarmee*. As had happened so often in the Eastern Campaign, here, too, the command of an army was outrageously usurped by a fool and a layman and, with open eyes, driven into the abyss.

At this time (25 January 1945) on the northern wing of the 2nd *Armee*, and, thus, of *Heeresgruppe 'Weichsel'* contact with *Heeresgruppe 'Nord'* in East Prussia was lost. A new *Kessel*, in addition to the one in Kurland, was formed. It would only be a matter of days before the third *Kessel* would be closed, cutting off the 2nd *Armee* in West Prussia.

The enemy situation left no possible doubt about the latter. In addition to the unchanging strong advance westward astride the Warthe River to the Oder and the attack on the Vistula front, it now became apparent that strong Russian forces would turn inward along the Schneidemühl –Deutsch-Krone line northward in the general direction of Neustettin. At that time the Russians constantly grew stronger overall against the *Heeresgruppe*. Despite the inadequate German aerial reconnaissance, great movements of troops and matériel were identified from the Kurland area and East Prussia. All of them were directed toward the Schneidemühl and Posen area. Enemy radio traffic also clearly indicated the appearance of numerous large formations and army staffs.

This invalidated Hitler's objective of fixing strong Russian forces by sacrificing the armies in Kurland and East Prussia. Even, however, at the last minute Hitler could not come to a decision to withdraw everything possible from those areas and thereby stiffen the wavering fronts of *Heeresgruppen 'Weichsel'* and *'Mitte'*. He resolutely held to the course that would most rapidly and certainly lead into the abyss.

Generaloberst Guderian had at that time tried every means to persuade Hitler to immediately evacuate Kurland and East Prussia, but to no avail. Here the difficult question must be raised as to whether he should have exposed himself to extreme personal danger and, throwing his position at Hitler's feet, offered his resignation. The overall situation must have made it clear to the Chief of the General Staff of the *Heer* that there was nothing left to save. Hitler's insane strategy, which did not offer even the slightest chance for success, could have been pursued just as well by any other stand-in. In this situation the fighting was no longer for Germany but for Hitler, himself, and with senseless, heavy bloody sacrifices. There can be doubt whether *Generaloberst* Guderian, whom Hitler had discharged at Moscow with calumny and shame, was in any way obligated to Hitler. His unforgettable name as the creator of the German armoured force and as an armoured commander in victorious battles gave deceptive hopes to many both at the front and at home.

The desperate situation of *Heeresgruppe 'Weichsel'* brought Himmler to the point of asking an immediate intervention by the *Führer*. The demand was for immediate provision of forces from the Kurland – East Prussia area. Otherwise the *Heeresgruppe* could not prevent catastrophe, neither for the 2nd *Armee* nor at the Oder. If such movement of those forces should be much delayed by unforeseeable circumstances, then it was requested that the 2nd *Armee* be shifted north to the 11th *SS Panzerarmee* in North Pomerania. That would require that West Prussia be evacuated, which could not, in any case, be held any longer with or without the 2nd *Armee*. With the 2nd *Armee*, however, the possibility remained of holding Pomerania and strengthening the Oder front, which was much too weak.

When I presented this proposal to Himmler and the Chief of the General Staff I held no hopes for a stabilization of the situation on a broad scale. At that point this was no longer possible, even if the 2nd *Armee* was brought in. I did, however, hope to free this large body of German soldiers that would hopelessly fall to the Russians in West Prussia from their grasp. No matter what the outcome of our fighting might be, in my opinion, the only objective now was to prevent yet more blood flowing in vain and to keep yet more German soldiers from falling into Russian hands. The Anglo-Americans were drawing ever closer to our backs. The day was approaching when, perhaps, the only decision left for the *Heeresgruppe* would be whether to surrender to the Western Powers or to the Russians. In that case only one decision would be possible.

It was, however, impossible at that time to present these simple considerations plainly and simply to Himmler's face. He was, however, convinced of the above respecting the defense of Pomerania and the Oder. In general, Himmler agreed, so far as it was possible for him to do so, that the situation was worsening. Himmler promised to do everything and, as so often before, drove to the *'Führerlage'*.

We held few hopes. When he returned, late in the evening, we immediately saw that something new was up, apparently, even, something positive. My skepticism was, however, already so great that I could not believe that Hitler had made a decisive decision in our favor.

That was correct. There was, however, something entirely new, as Himmler put it, an 'extremely great thing'. At last the time had arrived when the *Heeresgruppe* would deal the Russians a shattering blow. The *Führer* had, indeed, rejected all of our proposals, but (!!)... and now Himmler told this to myself and the Chief of staff with almost childlike zeal: A great *Panzerarmee* was immediately to be concentrated in the area east of Stettin. The *Heeresgruppe* would attack the rear of the Russian armoured forces assembled in the area north of Küstrin, destroy them and then – up to this point the matter still sounded entirely reasonable – now it became risky... The further objective would then be either the destruction of the enemy in the area south of the Warthe or a turn to the east against the rear of the enemy before the south flank of the 2nd *Armee* – thus, march direction approximately Bromberg – Thorn.

This was the surprise announcement of the fighting that would later be named the 'Battle of Stargard'.

Part VI

H itler required an immediate operations plan from the *Heeresgruppe* for this operation. Himmler was supposed to personally present this plan two days later. It was the task of the *Ia* to prepare it. In order to do so, above all else, it was necessary to get a statement from *OKH* as to what new armoured forces would be provided and when they would arrive at the *Heeresgruppe*? Himmler had made such imprecise statements regarding this most important question that during the night I sought immediate clarification of these matters from the *Operationsabteilung* of *OKH*. The insinuations promised much, but here the old saying, 'A sparrow in the hand and a dove on the roof' applied. Great caution was called for. Bitter experience had taught us much about promises from Hitler and *OKH*. With permission from Hitler, who wanted everything kept top secret, during that very night the *Oberquartiermeister* [logistics] and the *General des Transportwesens* [transport] of the *Heeresgruppe* were briefed on the general outlines of the operation, but only to the extent necessary. Thus both could begin to consider, and, in part initiate, their preparations that were essential for an operation of such magnitude. The Chief of the General Staff, Lammerding, took only a relatively small part in the preparation of such an important operation. At least initially he left all the work, especially the clarification of all questions that were obscure, to the *Ia*. Since the rest of the war, however, was still going on, the *Ia* would have very much appreciated some support from him.

During the night I learned from *OKH* what troops would be provided to the *Heeresgruppe* for the intended operation. As I remember they consisted of: The staff of XXXXV *Panzerkorps*, 10th *SS Panzerdivision 'Frundsberg'*, 4th *SS Polizei-Panzergrenadier Division,* 18th *Panzerdivision, Panzerdivision 'Holstein'*, *Führer-Begleit-* and *Führer-Grenadier Divisionen* (both *Panzer*-divisions). In addition to the above the III *(germanische) SS Panzerkorps* with its two stem-divisions *'Nordland'* and *'Nederland'* were named.

The armoured forces thus comprised two *Panzerkorps* with eight *Panzerdivisionen*. At first glance that would appear to be a considerable armoured force, particularly in light of the long-time exceedingly modest German situation. Somewhat later the *Heeresgruppe* was also told that the 1st *Panzer-Jagd-Brigade* would be forthcoming. Since I had not yet heard of such a unit I learned, after several inquiries, that it was a formation consisting of several *Sturmgeschütz-Abteilungen* and *Panzerjagdkommandos*. If all these armoured formations were at full strength there would have been a total of 1200-1500 armoured fighting vehicles. That would have amounted to the approximate armoured strength of a Russian tank army.

For the *Heeresgruppe* it was now a matter of finding out, as soon as possible, the condition of these *Panzer* divisions and their probable arrival times in the concentration area. About half of these units came from the sector adjoining to the *Heeresgruppe's* right, *Heeresgruppe Schörner*. Accordingly, I contacted its *Ia*, *Oberst i.G. Freiherr* von Weitershausen and requested more detailed information. What von Weitershausen told me in broad outlines certainly gave me cause to reflect. The units we were to receive from

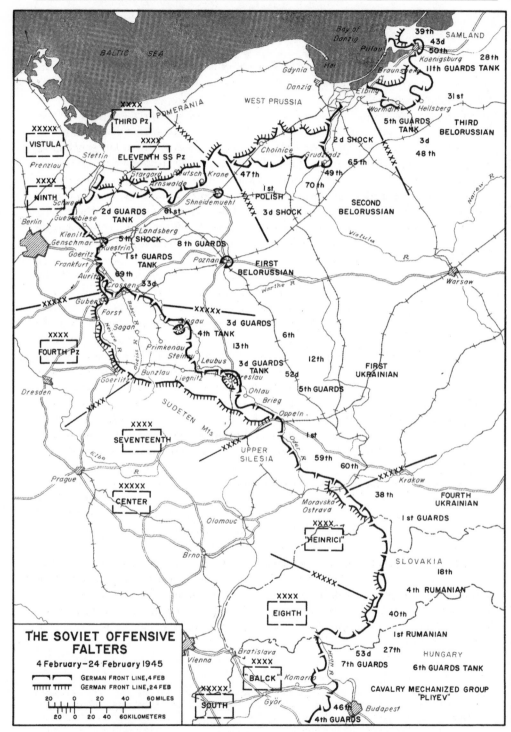

The Soviet Offensive Falters, 4-24 February 1945

our neighbour – 10th *SS Panzer-Division 'Frundsberg* and the two *Führer-* divisions, were supposed, as so nicely stated, to 'commencing immediately' be sent off to us by rail. However, the transport required a fairly lengthy period of time. The 18th *Panzer-Division* and *Panzer-Division 'Holstein'* were newly activated by *OKH*. They were supposed to come from training grounds somewhere. The 4th *SS Polizei-Division* was being reconstituted in the West.

When one realizes how many railway trains are needed for a *Panzer* division – in good times it required about 70; now, with the reduced strengths it still required 40 to 50 trains for each division – one can get a rough picture of the dimensions of the required rail-transport movement. This movement was particularly complicated by the relatively few serviceable railway networks suitable for the situation that were available. All movements first had to get through the Stettin bottleneck. Thus, the *General des Transportwesens* of the *Heeresgruppe, Oberst i.G.* Hamberger, had much to worry about since all of these additional and priority transports would endanger the ongoing logistical traffic in the *Heeresgruppe* sector. It can, however, be stated right from the start that he performed his onerous task superbly.

What was the situation of the individual divisions that were to come? *SS Panzer-Division 'Frundsberg'* was in the best state. It was nearly up to its full complement as a *Panzer*-division. The two newly activated units *'Holstein'* and 18th *Panzer-Division* were, as far as strengths of armour and also *Panzergrenadiere* went, actually to be counted as no more than *Panzer*-brigades. Each of these divisions was slated to have as its full complement only about 80 tanks or assault guns [*Sturmgeschütze*]. As for their *Panzergrenadiere* there were only one to two *GPW* (*Grenadierpanzerwagen)* companies [infantry companies mounted on lightly armoured half-track vehicles – *SPW, Schützenpanzerwagen*] instead of at least a full battalion.

So far as I remember, these divisions also had only one *Panzergrenadierregiment* with two battalions and one *Aufklärungsabteilung* [reconnaissance battalion]. The artillery was similarly weak – two light *Abteilungen*.1 The two *Führer* divisions were a bit stronger, but they, too, were actually only armoured brigades. Each of these two divisions was supposed to have an armoured strength of about 100 – 120 armoured fighting vehicles at full strength. *OKH* sent the *Heeresgruppe* reports on the organization and condition of the new troops that were to be sent. On closer examination these were, however, found to be outdated. Thus it soon became clear to us there would be no reliable picture of the condition of all these divisions until they actually arrived.

The operations plan that Hitler demanded – we gave it the code-name of *'Husarenritt'* [Hussar's Ride] – would therefore by pretty theoretical with regard to the actual available combat strengths. Now, it will be obvious even to any military layman that the scope of the objectives set for any operation always depends on the strength of the available friendly forces. In working out the plan I faced a mass of extremely decisive questions that could not be clarified.

---

1   Translator's note – The normal artillery regiment at the start of the war comprised four *Abteilungen*: three light *Abteilungen,* each with three four-gun batteries of 10.5 cm light field howitzers and a fourth heavy *Abteilung* with three four-gun batteries of 15 cm heavy field howitzers. The batteries were later reduced from four to three guns each.

The time for the start of the operation had to be set as soon as possible. The more the Russians gained in strength – and their strength mounted daily – the more limited must our objective be. Also, additional Russian successes in Pomerania and West Prussia would strongly influence the operation. In the event of a lengthy preparation period, that alone would mean that the planned assembly area around Stargard would be lost. Thus, its defense was vital. For this and a multitude of other reasons, the operation must be launched as soon as possible if there was to be any hope of any real success. The choice of the starting date, however, was not simply dependant on these dominating requirements, but exclusively based on the timely arrival of the formations involved and the essential preparation for and completion of their approach movements. The *Heeresgruppe* had practically no influence on these factors, since everything would be sent to it.

Despite the pressure of time, especially for a *Panzer* operation, the unconditionally necessary preparation time must be available. Otherwise such an operation is doomed from the start to be a half-baked thing that can, in the event, lead to nothing. A practical experience I had in 1942 was an advantage for me in this planning. It had to do with the fighting on the Crimean peninsula and the commitment of the newly activated and not yet entirely ready 22nd *Panzer-Division*. There, too, time pressed. The desire was, before the battle of Kertsch, to eliminate an extremely unfavorable salient in the front before the Russians could make further use of it. At that time nothing could move fast enough. Elements of this division went nearly directly from railroad car into combat. Commitment did not wait for the arrival of other elements of the division. The result was negative. The brand-new division was badly battered and required a great deal of time and care to be more-or-less restored to order. The appointed objective was not attained. I was, at that time, detailed from the 11th *Armee* to this division and had, thereby, learned a lot, especially about what not to do.

The operations plan that the *Heeresgruppe* presented to Hitler foresaw the attack of the 11th *SS Panzerarmee* from the area east of Stargard in a generally southwest direction with all available armoured forces and, so far as the situation allowed, any infantry forces that could be freed-up. Three attack groups were to be formed, with the center one strongest. It would be, one might say, the spearhead of the assault wedge. The other two had to cover the lengthening flanks. The eastern group, in particular, had to cover the ever-lengthening eastern flank of the attack as it progressed to the south. Based on the strengths of the friendly forces available a relatively limited objective was proposed, namely to advance to Küstrin with the left wing. If our forces were thus held tightly concentrated without squandering them it would be possible to cover our own exposed flank and smash the enemy forces to the north and northwest.

Hitler approved the basic plan, but the first objective for the extreme eastern wing was significantly shifted to the east, to Landsberg. He even dreamed of Kreuz. That would, indeed, be extremely desirable. The *Heeresgruppe* knew that, too. It would have preferred to deliver an attack on Posen. However, our forces simply were inadequate for that, and the enemy, who must also be taken into consideration, was far too strong for such a distant objective. Another important factor was that the *Panzer-* divisions had practically no infantry to work with the armour and take control of and ultimately mop up the terrain they captured. In addition, the ever-lengthening east flank must be screened unless one wanted to have the Russians force it inward and finally cut off the attacking force. And, it was exactly to the east that, according to all reconnaissance, steadily increasing pressure was to be expected from the enemy. Right from the start an extremely strong Russian counterattack had to be expected against the east flank of our attack. The talk of 'Panzer attack without concern for our own flank' could not apply in this situation unless one wanted to carelessly gamble the last usable armoured formations of the entire German *Wehrmacht* – that was what was at stake here.

For these reasons the *Heeresgruppe* believed that it had to limit the choice of objectives. Even the first objective that it had set, Küstrin, evoked serious reservations due to the lack of infantry. Himmler repeatedly pressed for at least two additional infantry divisions for this attack. Only with these could the *Panzer-* divisions be employed in a practical and concentrated manner. Without the infantry, a highly undesirable fragmentation of forces would be inevitable because the requisite screening of the flanks would have to be taken over by elements of the armoured assault force.

The employment of forces that Hitler desired and, finally, ordered was far too broad and would necessarily lead to fragmentation of the forces. I later discovered that *Generaloberst* Guderian, by the way, fully and completely supported Hitler's viewpoint, even though he was *the* armour-expert of the German *Heer*.

It has already been established that the date of the start of the attack would be decisive. Hitler and *OKH* also knew that. Accordingly the pushing and shoving began. According to the gradually accumulating facts the *Heeresgruppe* could see that it would be impossible to launch the attack in less than 14 days. The main reason for this was that the main body of the armoured formations simply would not be ready for action. Almost all would, indeed, arrive before that time in the concentration area. All, however, lacked elements vital for the impending heavy fighting. Some formations, such as the 4th *SS Polizei-Division* lacked entire troop elements. All, however, were lacking armoured fighting vehicles that *OKH* was supposed to furnish, in part from current production, which were needed to more-or-less fill out the armoured regiments.

This was a matter of significant numbers of armoured vehicles. Five of the eight divisions still needed 25-30 more armoured fighting vehicles each. That amounted to nearly half of the entire complement. The *Heeresgruppe* could not do without these allotments of armour under any circumstances. They had to be there and, indeed, be effectively integrated before the attack could begin. The man who was, at that time, specially assigned by Hitler to matters concerning armour, *Generalleutnant* Thomale, did, indeed, promise everything and always immediately. In the event, however, he needed a lot of time and could not entirely fulfil his promises.

In this irritating give-and-take it became ever clearer to me that this entire operation was doomed to failure. The forces were, of themselves, inadequate and the delayed onset of the operation deprived it of any chance of success. Finally, the commitment of the last mobile troops of the German *Heer* in this operation was not in any way justified by the anticipated local success with major losses.

I expressed these views both to the Chief of the General Staff and to Himmler. But what could one do against the almighty order from Hitler? Himmler did, however, realize that, at least, all the preparations had to be completed. He, too, did not want to let himself be involved in a dubious adventure. The time required to prepare the armoured formations was thoroughly discussed with the Commander in Chief of the 11th *SS Panzerarmee* as well as with the Commanding Generals of the *Panzerkorps* and with most of the division commanders. All shared the same opinion that the attack could not begin before the arrival of the last of the armour. Most of these men, however, were convinced that the entire attack would be a failure. Such was the state of things when the Chief of the General Staff of the *Heer*, *Generaloberst* Guderian, as ordered by Hittler, set the day of the attack as 15 February 1945. It was clearly apparent that the necessary preparations would be far from completion upon that date.

Two additional factors came up that also weighed in against carrying out the operation. The first was that discussions with the *Oberquartiermeister* of the *Heeresgruppe* regarding necessary logistical support of the troops for the attack revealed that there was not enough fuel available. Despite all discussions with the *OKH Generalquartiermeister*, the *Heeresgruppe Oberquartiermeister, Oberst i.G.* von Rücker, reported that, for the planned number of vehicles of the *Panzer*-divisions there was only enough fuel for about three to four days and that, from his experience and what he knew of what *OKH* was capable of, there could be no assurance of timely provision of supplies after those three days.

That in itself should well have been conclusive grounds for cancelling the operation. The most recent past provided examples of large-scale armoured operations being brought to a standstill as a result of lack of fuel. In the Ardennes Offensive the attack finally had to be halted because of fuel shortages and, instead of the hoped-for grand success, it turned into a major defeat in the West. Now the same mistake was about to be repeated here. The ammunition situation looked nearly as bad. I can no longer remember exact numbers, but I know that, especially with regard to the critical special ammunition for the armour, there was a serious shortage. It was predictable that it would be impossible to make good the high expenditure of ammunition which experience had shown could be expected in such an armoured battle. Thereby the necessary fundamental prerequisites for carrying out the operation were missing.

In addition, bad, wet weather set in just before the start of the attack. The terrain for the attack – not what you would call dry at best – would thus be extremely difficult for the armoured vehicles, if not completely impassable. One thing was immediately obvious: the armour would generally be tied to the extremely narrow and poor network of roads and highways. Thus the armoured attack would be channeled The very strength of the armour, its mobility over the terrain, would be severely restricted. Here, too, there was a precedent from the preceding year of the war: The 6th *SS Panzerarmee* under *Obergruppenführer* Sepp Dietrich bogged down in the mud during its relief attack on Budapest. In our case the isthmus between the Platten-See [lake] and Velence-See in Hungary was replaced by that between Madue-See and Plöne-See, resulting in a very similar situation.

Himmler could not ignore these numerous grave problems and demanded from *OKH*, above all, a date for the attack that would permit completion of the most necessary preparations. Hitler and *OKH*, however, were all fired up. *Generaloberst* Guderian himself urged daily and accused *Heeresgruppe 'Weichsel'* of being sluggish and hesitant. He asserted that it wanted to sabotage the entire operation upon which the fate of the Eastern Front depended. This developed into an ongoing clash with *OKH* which gradually took an extremely bitter form. During a radio conversation with *Generaloberst* Guderian I had to repeatedly express serious reservations regarding the time set for the attack and the, as yet, incomplete preparations. That drew a reprimand that made the microphone vibrate. It ended with *Generaloberst* Guderian telling me that he would hold

General der Panzertruppe Walther Wenck, a photograph taken in 1943. In his capacity as Deputy Chief of the General Staff of the *Heer* he was assigned to *Heeresgruppe 'Weichsel'* to co-ordinate the Stargard operation, February 1945. On 7 April 1945 he was appointed CO 12. *Armee*, often known as *Armee Wenck*. (Bundesarchiv 101I-237-1051-15A)

me personally responsible for unconditionally carrying out all orders and for having the *Heeresgruppe* ready on the appointed date set for the attack. If the *Heeresgruppe* continued to work so slowly he would yank me out of the general staff. During the Chief of the General Staff's tirade all I could get in was an occasional *'Jawohl'*. At the end I informed him that I was merely the First General Staff Officer of the *Heeresgruppe*. Responsibility rested with the Commander in Chief. He again shouted at me that he would hold me responsible for everything. I was the First General Staff Officer of this *Heeresgruppe* and had to influence my Commander in Chief and Chief of the General Staff in whatever way he and *OKH* considered proper.

I felt obligated to immediate report to Himmler regarding this extremely bitter set-to. Himmler was furious and assured me that I was directly responsible to him and him alone. He would not permit any more interference in the rights and duties of the *Heeresgruppe*. He immediately contacted Guderian and made clear to him his views. In this conversation an immediate conference was set up with *Generaloberst* Guderian at the *Heeresgruppe*. It must be added that the distrust of the *Heeresgruppe* at *OKH* found expression in assignment of the Deputy Chief of the General Staff of the *Heer*, *Generalleutnant* Wenck, to the *Heeresgruppe* a few days later. His assignment was to advise the Commander in Chief and support the Chief of the *Heeresgruppe* general staff.

I knew *Generalleutnant* Wenck well from the time of the Battle of Stalingrad and as *Armee-* and *Heeresgruppe* chief of general staff. As a result of his great abilities and accomplishments he had enjoyed an extraordinarily rapid rise in his career. Whenever I had interacted with him in his official duties he impressed me as one of the most capable chiefs of general staff that we had anywhere at that time. His great strengths were, along with his sharp, clear understanding and insight into operational questions, his unique alertness, energy and resilience, coupled with unshakeable calm and an unfailing sense of humour even in the most difficult situations.

I was, therefore, exceedingly fortunate that this man was the Deputy Chief of the General Staff of the *Heer* upon my arrival as *Ia* of the *Heeresgruppe*. I held high hopes regarding his influence upon the Supreme Command. However, in the course of the first few weeks I received the impression that this influence was not that great. This impression, however, did not come so much from the few times that *Generalleutnant* Wenck spoke with me on the telephone, as from the development of the overall situation. Now, however, *Generalleutnant* Wenck was present in person at the *Heeresgruppe* and again one could hope for his support. Since he was an old, experienced *Panzer* man one could count on his sound judgement in the current controversy regarding the armoured battle of Stargard. Initially it must be stated that *Generalleutnant* Wenck no longer had quite the fiery spirit that one had previously known him for. He had aged considerably and frequently appeared to be completely exhausted. That was not surprising considering the burden that he had born for years and, most recently, in his current position.

He discussed quite openly with me the operations plan and its possibilities. In so doing he admitted to me a whole series of serious objections and reservations. Basically, however, he insisted that the attack take place at any price and as soon as possible. He personally drove around a great deal to the arriving *Panzer*-divisions, oriented himself in the terrain of the attack, talked with the division commanders and exhibited notable activity, if not to say unrest. It seemed as if he wanted to gain confidence at the front and among the troops in an operation that, deep inside, he could not believe in as a result of his own experience and expertise. On these drives – mostly alone on a motorcycle – it was not just positive and confident expressions that he heard, and which he then passed on to Himmler. He also saw great difficulties. Above all he doubtless saw that the appointed date for the start of the attack simply could not be met. The troops, who were still lacking so much, could not be ready.

After the discussion between Himmler and Guderian (14 February 1945) in which, after long and quite energetic objections from Himmler, Guderian had finally prevailed, with reference to Hitler's hopes, Guderian came to Wenck's room, where I remained. *Generaloberst* Guderian appeared to be completely worn out as a result of his stubborn battle with Himmler. Here, yet again, he implored both Wenck and I, too, to set everything at stake in order to launch the attack upon the appointed date. This, time, however, it was no harsh order but the imploring request of a man who was nearly at the end of his strength. It made a deep impression on me. It was now apparent that even this man had been broken by Hitler.

Nevertheless, *Generalleutnant* Wenck expressed with all clarity his serious reservations regarding the start of the attack, which he sought to substantiate with his own experiences and discoveries at the front with the troops. *Generaloberst* Guderian wanted to hear nothing of it. When Wenck said that, in that case, he would be in the wrong place here at the *Heeresgruppe* and requested his recall, Guderian only replied: 'The attack must be carried through. Everything depends on it.' So far as *OKH* was concerned, that was its final word and fate must run its course.

Following this discussion *Generalleutnant* Wenck was seriously depressed. The following day he had an accident on his drive to the troops with the motorcycle and was hospitalized. He took no more part in this controversial attack, for which he was initially so enthusiastic and whose success he finally doubted. It is significant that, after the complete failure of the operation, Hitler said: 'If Wenck had been there it could not have failed.' However, let us not get ahead of events.

As ordered, the attack was launched on 15 February 1945. Some of the armour that *OKH* had promised had not yet arrived. Another part of the promised armour was sent into battle direct from the railroad cars without adjustment of the sights of the guns or inspection of the vehicles. In the event things turned out in every detail exactly as the *Heeresgruppe* had predicted. The great attack gained about eight kilometers of ground, then bogged down in the mud and in the face of increasing enemy resistance. The fighting around Stargard lasted about two days without gaining any success at all. Two more days were spent trying to get the armoured attack rolling again, but to no avail.

Instead of the anticipated destruction of the Russian tank armies, we suffered significant losses in men and matériel. The armoured formations were pulled back again into their assembly areas. Closely pursued by the Russians, the weak infantry forces were unable even to hold their jump-off positions. The front was forced back east of Stargard to the general line Arnswalde – southern tip of Medue-See. A whole series of localities were also lost south of Stettin. Here the front extended from the northern tip of Madue-See to the Oder River.

Part VII

During roughly this same period *Heeresgruppe 'Schörner'* suffered serious setbacks in Silesia. The enemy reached the Lausitzer Neiße River. Hitler and *OKH* resolved to regroup anew the armoured forces in order to help this *Heeresgruppe*. Accordingly, the main bodies of all the *Panzer-* divisions were sent off to *Heeresgruppe 'Mitte'* over the same route via Stettin by which they had come. *Heeresgruppe 'Weichsel'* retained only III *SS Panzerkorps* with its divisions *'Nordland'* and *'Nederland'*, both of which, actually, barely amounted to regiments, and the 4th *SS Polizei-Division*.

In the meantime the staff of the 3rd *Panzerarmee* was sent to *Heeresgruppe 'Weichsel'*. That rendered the newly-activated staff of the 11th *SS Panzerarmee* superfluous. *Obergruppenführer* Steiner turned over command of his army to the 3rd *Panzerarmee* under *Generaloberst* Raus. He, himself, and his staff received as their new assignment the registration- and receiving-organization in the rear area of the *Heeresgruppe*. This consisted of a strictly run and centrally controlled registration of all superfluous replacement elements and the collection of the ever-increasing number of stragglers. At that time the confusion in this area was like a veritable Babel. The efforts of Steiner, who tackled this task with a great deal of energy and vigour, made obvious the entirely unacceptable command and subordination relationships in the *Heimatskriegsgebiet* [homeland-war-area]. In this area the *Gauleiters* ruled as they had before as *Reichsverteidigungskommissare* [*Reichs*-defense commissars]. Just the territory of *Heeresgruppe 'Weichsel'* included the following *Gaue* [provinces or districts]: Brandenburg, Mecklenburg, Pomerania and West Prussia. Important matters required constant negotiation with these four 'great lords of the party'. They all still had their ambition, though this steadily lessened as the front grew nearer.

In the military realm this ambition spent itself in the activation of the *Volkssturm* and in the construction of numerous rear positions and obstacles. Both the rear positions and the innumerable obstacles were, almost without exception, nonsensical. Each *Gauleiter* did as he thought fit without any sort of consultation with his neighbour. The military advisors of the *Gaue* did not advise too happily in these matters. Above all else senseless anti-tank ditches, which were generally only usable for weekly newsreel takes, were dug in profusion. In the entire war I had have never seen an anti-tank ditch, neither our own nor the enemy's, that seriously interfered with an armoured attack. These anti-tank ditches and the felled-tree and timber obstacles on the roads had to be removed or blown up by our own troops because they interfered intolerably with the traffic of troops and supplies. What a tremendous amount of self-sacrificing, heavy work by the civilians, especially by German women, was wasted here! Near Stettin I saw columns of women and girls building positions. Here the *Gau* government was, at last, eliminated from the process and something useful was produced. The *Gau* governments proved equally incapable in traffic-control organizations on the roads and streets. There, too, everyone worked at cross-purposes. As long as part of the *Gau* was in the immediate front area these conditions remained in effect. Repeated attempts, even by Himmler, to get these relationships changed through Hitler failed. The party hung on desperately to the remnants of its power – here in an entirely false position. The *Gauleiter* had, indeed, vital duties and tasks respecting the population of their own *Gaue* and, especially, also for the refugees from neighbouring *Gaue*. What was needed was not pompous, bombastic calls to fight to the last man but practical, well thought out assistance.

The chapter of the evacuation and withdrawal of the refugees from the German East will always remain one of the blackest chapters in the dark history of the party leadership. In this vital matter of evacuation the party could have, as it is said, 'proved itself' by demonstrating that it could master difficult problems with energy and skill, not in times of surplus and good fortune, but especially in times of bitter consequence and need. Here that phrase which had been used-to-death, 'true *Volks* brotherhood' could have been proven in action. When, however, the call for 'political leaders to the front' rang forth, those leaders failed to a man, from *Gauleiter* down to block-warden, with a few praiseworthy exceptions. It must be stated that a large part of the burden of heavy guilt with respect to refugees and exiles falls on Hitler himself.

For reasons of pure prestige, he forbad the timely evacuation of East Prussia, West Prussia and Posen. There are countless known examples where the populations of cities and villages only received the call to immediately evacuate their homes a few hours before the arrival of the enemy. There can be no talk of any orderly preparation for such a modern diaspora. Generally the people were neither given opportunity to prepare to bring their most vital possessions with them nor was adequate thought given to possible transportation and supply. Indeed, not even the so-urgently-required traffic control functioned. Here the traffic to and from the front and the refugee traffic often resulted in mass confusion until, finally, the troops helped. In Silesia there was, initially, a sort of march regulation. In West Prussia and Pomerania, on the other hand, there was not a trace of traffic control. The *Gau* government failed almost totally with respect to basic instructions. How could the little local group leaders do any better? The unspeakable misery that resulted from this traitorous inactivity will probably never be fully known.

The mass deaths of old people, women and children on the great trek-routes of Pomerania were witnessed by all who were there at that time. As a result of march orders that were issued far too late the majority of the treks were literally rolled over by the Russians, and, indeed, by tanks![1] For the majority of the refugees, the result of the over-late calls for evacuation were far worse than it would have been to await the enemy in their homes. However, the inhuman bestial rage of the Red Army in our Eastern territories must be considered. These spots will never be washed from the shield of this army. The saying is not in vain that: 'The plague of bloody vengeance goes ever onward.'

Every German soldier who fought in the East in Russia, whether during the advance or the retreat, will support me in saying that he never saw the German *Wehrmacht* engage in this sort of unbelievable crime – here the new expression 'crimes against humanity' surely fits. These Russian deeds can, today, be attested to a thousand-fold. What was perpetrated here, above all against German woman and girls, from the gray-haired to the little children, can never be justified, not even by vengeance and retribution. Here the Red Army exhibited behaviour that had hitherto only appeared in world history

1   Translator's note – For the average modern reader, even the words the author used lack sufficient emphasis. In actual fact, time and time again Russian tanks literally ran over and crushed columns of German civilian refugees, squashing the human beings and their possessions.

to this extent with the conquering Mongol armies of Genghis Khan and Tamerlane. I am not certain whether the Thirty Years War, as so graphically described to us by Grimmelshausen in his *Simplizissimus* can stand in comparison.[2]

Finally I must say that I have never had such a feeling of immense shame, helplessness and sadness in the entire war as a German soldier as that which I felt at the sight of the refugee treks. Never was I more clearly aware of the entire excessive present and future misery of our once great and proud German people. I suspect that it was exactly the same for every one of my comrades.

Following the withdrawal of the staff of the 11th *SS Panzerarmee Heeresgruppe 'Weichsel'* had the following organization:

The 9th *Armee* was at the Oder Front, from the mouth of the Lausitzer Neiße River to the Hohenzollern Canal. The 3rd *Panzerarmee* was at the Oder Front from the Hohenzollern Canal to south of Greifenhagen, then in the line Madue-See – Stargard – Arnswalde – Falkenburg – Neustettin – Hammerstein. The 2nd *Armee* adjoined and continued via Zempelburg – Schwetz, the Vistula – Nogat – Elbing. The front thus extended about 450 kilometers. It had nearly doubled in length since the time when the *Heeresgruppe* assumed command without anything like a commensurate increase in troop strength. The front was, thus, vastly overextended. Within the immediate future it would tear apart in several places. The Russians facing the Oder Front had come to a rather stable state. They were concentrating according to plan. Reconnaissance confirmed that beyond possible doubt. They were already, however, making initial local advances over the river. Here the enemy wanted to infiltrate and build small bridgeheads that later could easily be enlarged. Accordingly the 9th *Armee* had a certain amount of time to prepare, as much as was possible, for the expected major Russian offensive. Essentially these preparations consisted of developing the necessary depth in the main defensive area. Even though there were no troops available for its immediate manning – the river front was already held but thinly – the troops nevertheless prepared new systems of positions to which they could later cling. On the 9th *Armee* front German bridgeheads were still held near the fortresses of Frankfurt-an-der-Oder and Küstrin. These cities were strengthened with all available means, but those means were pretty wretched.

The same calm before the storm reigned at that time on the Oder Front of the 3rd *Panzerarmee*. Here German bridgeheads were held near Schwedt and Greifenhagen. The enemy limited himself on this front to pure reconnaissance. Similar calm held between the Oder River and Madu-See.

The situation was very different on the inner wings of the 3rd *Panzerarmee* and 2nd *Armee*. Here X *SS Korps*, in particular, had been under heavy attacks for days on both sides of the Falkenburg lake-plain [*Seenplatte*]. Thereby two Russian *Schwerpunkte* were evident: The one was in the area north of Arnswalde – this city was encircled – the other was in the Neustettin area. The Russians appeared to intend a twofold breakthrough to the Baltic coast in the general direction of Kolberg – Köslin. That would eliminate the

---

2   Translator's note – Here the author is alluding to one of the greatest German novels of the 17th Century, *Der abenteuerliche Simplicissimus Teutsch, d.h. die Beschreibung des Lebens eines seltsamen Vaganten, genannt Melchior Sternfels von Fuchsheim*, written by Hans Jakob Christoffel von Grimmelshausen and published in 1668. In it, the author describes in fictitious form the adventures of the book's hero through the destruction of the Thirty Years War. The author himself had first-hand experience of much of what he wrote.

center of the *Heeresgruppe*. One would then expect the operation to continue with strong Russian forces turning against the area northeast of Stettin, on the one hand and, on the other, in the rear of the 2nd *Armee* in the area west of Danzig. The time had now come for the irretrievable last possibility to bring in the 2nd *Armee* and thereby save it from an increasingly obviously developing *Kessel*. For the umpteenth time I urged the Chief of the General Staff of the *Heeresgruppe* to get such a decision from Himmler and send it, yet again, to Hitler – to no avail.

Himmler had lost yet more ground as a result of the failed armoured battle near Stargard, even though he had attempted to prevent this battle. Although *OKH*, and especially *Generaloberst* Guderian were careful to cast no open aspersions on Himmler, since the *Heeresgruppe* had been all too clearly correct with its warnings, it was still plain to all that Himmler was to be the necessary whipping boy. Because of this strained relationship with Hitler, Himmler dared nothing at the time. In an effort to, at least, save something, I proposed that the two armoured divisions with the 2nd *Armee*, the 7th *Panzerdivision* and 4th *Panzerdivision* be transferred immediately to the 3rd *Panzerarmee* in the Belgard area in Pomerania, thus behind its left wing. The reasoning for this follows:

The Russian breakthrough to the Baltic and, thereby, the encirclement of the 2nd *Armee* was inevitable. Sooner or later this army was going to be compressed into a bridgehead around Danzig. What possible use could these two valuable mobile divisions be there? The battle in Pomerania and at the Oder, on the other hand, would continue. There these divisions could be employed effectively in accord with their special capabilities. From Belgard, southeast of Kolberg, southwest of Köslin, approximately at the apex of an inverted equilateral triangle with Kolberg and Köslin at the other two apices they could be employed to good effect either against the enemy thrust toward Köslin or against the thrust toward Kolberg, hopefully against the flank but, at the least, against the armoured spearhead. Here they would not be cut off but, instead, could always be withdrawn to Stettin.

In any case a mobile combat force belonged behind the site of the anticipated enemy breakthrough. Even *OKH* realized that and, far too late, had thrown the entirely too-weak *Panzerdivision 'Holstein'* in there. By employing this division in conjunction with the two above-mentioned *Panzer*-divisions the 2nd *Armee* would have been able to do decisive damage to the spearheads of the Russian breakthrough in open country in mobile combat.

However, this proposal, too, was not accepted. And so happened what had to happen. The enemy broke through the weak front of X *SS Korps* at both of the anticipated places and encircled the main body of this *Korps* in the Dramburg – Labes area. Simultaneously Russian armour advanced toward Kolberg and Köslin. Near Stargard the now cut-off east wing of the 3rd *Panzerarmee* hung in the air in the face of strong enemy attacks. The Russians could go wherever they desired in all of Eastern Pomerania [*Hinterpommern*]. There was no resistance of any sort to be found there. There was just thin air.

Initially the *Heeresgruppe* had no information regarding the situation of X *SS Korps* in the area of the breakthrough. The last radio messages from this *Korps* from the Dramburg area confirmed the double Russian breakthrough. The troops of this *Korps* were a particularly makeshift lot. The core element was the 5th *Jäger Division*, which was, in fact, the only regular unit. All the rest were newly activated units of limited combat value without firm structure but with the deceptive designation as divisions. Included was *'Division Bärwalde'*, formed from the *Fahnenjunkerschule* I for artillery.[3] Comprising the highest grade of human material, these *Fahnenjunker* performed at a level beyond all praise despite inadequate weapons and leadership. Plucked right out of their lecture-rooms and thrown into the *'Bärwalde* Position' – an inadequately prepared rear-position on both sides of Bärwalde – with heavy bloody losses they presented a shining example of the German soldier at his best during the odyssey of the remnants of X *SS Korps*. As a general of this breakout-group later told me, these *Fahnenjunker* youngsters were often the example and stimulus for combat-experienced troops. The *Korps* also included two so-called *'Nr. – Divisionen'* formed from alarm-units.

It was only from the Russian radio news broadcasts that we first learned what happened to X *SS Korps* after it was cut off on 3 March. These broadcasts made known the encirclement and destruction of the *Korps* in the Labes area, and the capture of its Commanding General, *Generalleutnant* Krappe. Particular mention should be made of the fact that *Generalleutnant* Krappe, my old peacetime battalion commander fell into Russian hands, wounded, on his own estate, Schilde, near Dramburg. Thus he defended his Pomeranian homeland, fighting to the last on its ground, true to the end. The remnants of his *Korps* finally fought their way through the midst of the Russian forces to Wollin after eventful fighting.

These events basically altered the situation of the *Heeresgruppe*. The worst complication was the effect of division into two separate parts upon further conduct of the battle. It grew increasingly difficult to command the special-combat-theater [*Sonderkriegschauplatz*] of West Prussia, meaning the 2nd *Armee*. There was still a telephone connection by undersea cable, but now the entire logistical support had to be by sea, as was the case with Kurland and East Prussia. It soon became evident that the combat in the 2nd *Armee* sector had scarcely any influence on the primary sector of the *Heeresgruppe*.

As the fighting in Kurland and East Prussia gradually drew to a close, the enemy freed up so many forces that he could draw the ring around West Prussia tighter without interfering with the orderly preparation for his great blow against Berlin. Particularly depressing was the fact that it was no longer possible to help the 2nd *Armee*. Again and again the purely factual daily situation-reports included the justified complaint from this brave army: "You left us in the lurch. You have had neither enough courage nor sense of responsibility to spare us from this sorry fate, even though it would have been to your own advantage so to do."

In this situation one could, at least, have expected that the Commander in Chief or the Chief of the General Staff of the *Heeresgruppe* would have flown to the 2nd *Armee*. It would not have been especially hazardous to have, at least, made an appearance to demonstrate that, despite the separation, the *Heeresgruppe* was still in contact and would remain in contact with the 2nd *Armee*. Granted, it would have given no material aid, but it would have been an obvious duty to an honourable soldier. Himmler and Lammerding, however, were not up to it. It was deeply shameful of them and showed the slipshod attitude of these leaders. I have deeply reproached myself that I did not do

---

3 Translator's note – Officer-candidate school. The *Fahnenjunker* was the initial stage as an officer candidate, before promotion to *Fähnrich*.

this either. At the time I did, indeed, have so much to do that I could hardly leave the *Heeresgruppe* headquarters for a single hour. There was too much pressure on us and the necessary work did, indeed, have to be done. I can only hope, today, that the command at that time of the 2nd *Armee* understood. They knew the situation.

Himmler spoke, as often as possible, with *Generaloberst* Weiß. He pulled out all stops so far as gracious and commendatory words could go, but it sounded like a mockery of the slow death of this army. In this regard I cannot forget a radio interchange between Himmler and Hitler. Hitler did not like radio conversations, as he had been somewhat hard of hearing since the assassination attempt. In the course of the ongoing conversation – it had to do with the evacuation of Elbing, which had cost the 2nd *Armee* hecatombs of blood – Himmler said that *Generaloberst* Weiß had described the Elbing situation as having been untenable. Thereupon the deep, somewhat tired voice of Hitler's responded: "Weiß lies like all generals". I listened to this, as to so many other conversations, on a second handset. This brief statement of Hitler's characterized better than lengthy discourses his fundamental attitude toward the generals. It must be stated that *Generaloberst* Weiß's report was entirely in accord with the facts.

The more unfavorable the situation of *Heeresgruppe* 'Weichsel' became, the greater Himmler's loss, as responsible Commander in Chief, of influence at *Führer*-headquarters. People, in general, had developed a false impression of this man's power. Generally, in Germany and abroad, people thought that this 'Fouchee'[4] had gradually risen to a position second to Hitler in the Third *Reich*. He was the *Reichsführer-SS*, Chief of the German Police, Interior Minister and Commander-in-Chief of the Reserve Army [*Ersatzheer*]. Thus he held the entire control of interior Germany in his hand. As mentioned earlier, he remained, to the very last, one of Hitler's closest and most trusted intimates. It must be conceded that a genuine person of some stature with these offices could, indeed, have been the mightiest of the dictator's paladins. Such a man could well have been the actual power behind the scenes. Himmler did not have that stature. Despite all the external power he remained the 'young man' in his relationship with Hitler, who obediently snapped to attention when the *Führer* issued orders. Nor could he prevail against the other 'greats' of the Third *Reich*. Bormann and Göring, perhaps Ley, too, were more significant. Himmler seemed to realize that. His relationships with these three men appeared externally friendly. In actual fact they were rivals. In this rivalry the other three were ahead of him, especially Bormann.

His entire powerlessness was finally demonstrated by what he failed to accomplish as Commander in Chief of *Heeresgruppe* 'Weichsel' despite his numerous influential positions. As Commander in Chief of the Replacement Army he was unable to prevail and get

4　Translator's note – Joseph Fouché (1759 or 1763 – 1820) was an opportunist, intriguer and survivor – and politician without apparent morals. During the French Revolution he shifted positions and affiliations adeptly, supported the Reign of Terror and assisted in the ruthless 1793 massacre of counter-revolutionists in Lyon. He became minister of police in 1799, but then assisted Napoleon Bonaparte's 18e Brumaire (9–10 November, 1799). Constantly intriguing and shifting sides, repeatedly dismissed, yet reappearing, the positions he held varied, as did his relationship with the current regime. The Columbia Encyclopedia (© 2001-07, Columbia University Press) described him as "One of the indispensable men of the Napoleonic empire, Fouché is sometimes considered the father of the modern police state; nevertheless, his reforms of the criminal police were a lasting achievment." He died in obscure exile in Trieste.

timely and appropriate replacements in men and matériel for his own *Heeresgruppe*, even though it would have been possible. His deputy in this position, *SS Obergruppenführer* Jüttner, an elderly, morose and unsoldierly man was a complete failure. He had neither the requisite energy nor the proper grasp, to say nothing of the necessary knowledge. Thus the powerful Commander in Chief of the Replacement Army, himself, experienced how it went with Commanders in Chief who urgently sought replacements and received none. In this case it could no longer have been any sort of sabotage by the traitors of 20 July [the conspiracy to assassinate Hitler]. Himmler, himself, had indeed bragged that he would finally bring order to the Replacement Army. One had only to reread his great speech on assuming that office.

The same held true for Himmler's possibilities as Interior Minister. He was unable to put through a single one of his proposed measures to provide new regulation of the powers of the *Gauleiters*] and the military command. He accomplished nothing regarding evacuation and withdrawal of populations of areas of Germany soon to be conquered by the Russians.

Finally, he remained the almighty, feared Chief of the Police. It was impossible to see how he exercised his power in that area from the context of the *Heeresgruppe*. There were, however, signs that he was not altogether lord of this sector. Himmler's deputy in that office, Kaltenbrunner, later to be executed, did not appear to get along too well with Himmler. In general, as far as one could see, Himmler was unsuccessful in selecting his fellow workers.

There were actually only two of his budding field-generals of the *Waffen-SS* who were talented men: They were *Oberstgruppenführer* Hauser and *Obergruppenführer* Steiner. The other so-called *Armee* – commanders and Commanding Generals [*Korps* commanders] of the *Waffen-SS* were, without exception, failures. During his time as Commander in Chief of the *Heeresgruppe*, Himmler, himself, relieved *SS Obergruppenführer* Demlhuber, von Bachcelewsky [*sic.,* von dem Bach–Zelewski], Krüger and *SS Gruppenführer* Reinefarth for incompetence and replaced them by generals from the *Heer* [army].

Himmler made a particularly unfortunate selection in his *SS Adjutant* with Hitler, *Gruppenführer und Generalleutnant der Waffen-SS* Fegelein. This man had risen from an exalted stable-boy to general. He owed his meteoric-like rise in the *Waffen-SS* to his deeds as commander of an *SS* cavalry regiment and, later, an *SS* cavalry division in the East. There, for a quite short time, he displayed indubitable courage and daring. He understood nothing of military command. He was, however, the most lying and evil intriguer whom I ever experienced during this war. He had his filthy fingers into everything. His unashamed arrogant conduct toward older, experienced men was unparalleled. Even toward Himmler, with whom he was familiar [using the intimate pronoun, *du*], he employed a tone in private which was, at the very least, remarkable.

In the course of time both Lammerding and I discovered that Fegelein calumniated Himmler in the worst possible way with Hitler. He often passed on the most lying reports regarding the situation of the *Heeresgruppe* that were none of his business.

Now Lammerding felt outspoken anxiety before the almighty Fegelein. I often experienced this during phone calls that I had to listen in on.[5] The repulsive, emphatically

---

5   Translator's note – It was standard practice to have a second responsible person listen in on important conversations over a second phone to ensure accurate understanding.

sharp voice of Fegelein generally opened with: "The *Führer* demands immediately at today's situation-briefing this or that triviality". Then Lammerding would usually go to pieces. Finally, as Fegelein's trouble-making worsened steadily I persuaded Lammerding to tell Himmler the plain truth about his friend. After several protests, Himmler agreed that Fegelein was out of line. He was unwilling, however, to recall him, even though Fegelein's behaviour was causing him real harm. Fegelein met a well-deserved end. When he attempted to flee from the *Reichs* chancellery [as the Russians closed in during the final fighting in Berlin] his brother-in-law, Hitler, stood him up against the wall [and had him shot], after first stripping him of all his orders and awards.

Part VIII

After the *Heeresgruppe* was split in two signs increasingly pointed to a major Russian offensive over the Oder for an advance on Berlin. During the time of the Russian preparations *Reichsmarschall* Hermann Göring was a constant visitor to the staff of the *Heeresgruppe*. Granted, aside from a special *Staffel* [squadron, 9-12 planes] under the renowned *Stuka* pilot, *Oberstleutnant* Baumbach, there was essentially no more *Luftwaffe* supporting our battle. The mission of this *Staffel* was the ongoing destruction of the various Russian bridges and crossings over the Oder. More will be said later regarding its activity.

Nevertheless, there was no hiding the particularly active interest of the *Herr Reichsmarschall* in our sector. He, himself, explained that it was primarily that two of his best *Fallschirmjäger* divisions, as I remember the 5th and 9th, were committed with *Heeresgruppe 'Weichsel'*. The 9th was in the Küstrin area, the 5th south of Stettin. Unfriendly tongues, however, attributed these notable visits to Goering's concern that Karinhall – he was living there at the time – was under immediate threat. Accordingly he wanted to defend it with the entire weight of his personality. These allegations were, undoubtedly, exaggerated, but there may well have been some truth in them. At that time Göring impressed me as a man who was not entirely in control of himself and was in some way spiritually and morally disturbed. His entire being was overexcited volatility. His arrival was, as I had always experienced it, here, too, richly theatrical. Himmler behaved toward him with extreme amiability and courtesy, even though it was known that neither cared for the other. Himmler generally addressed Göring as *'Herr Reichsmarschall'* rather than as *'Parteigenosse* [party-comrade] Göring'. Himmler generally addressed the other party big-wigs with the latter. With Bormann, however, it was *'Lieber* [dear] *Martin'*. With Bormann Himmler used the familiar *'Du'*. However, here too, despite the *'Du'*, there was little mutual respect.

In his first visits Göring held sort of a situation briefing in Himmler's office with the Chief of Staff and *Ia* usually present. In general Göring delivered a monologue in his typical stance, supported by both arms, wide apart on the map table, moving his fat hands, ornamented with truly gigantic rings, in lively fashion around the map, pounding places that seemed particularly important to him with his fist. His so-called strategic insights were more in the nature of purposeful optimism. One could, then, only talk of wishful thinking. He considered that the Russians were, fundamentally, unworthy opponents who fled immediately if one was properly aggressive. He dismissed our data regarding the strength of enemy armour, which were supported by detailed reconnaissance and surveillance, with a wave of his hand as greatly exaggerated. It was quite obvious that, on the one hand, he was unable to comprehend the true situation on our front because of insufficient knowledge and, on the other hand, he did not want to recognize the truth as it now really existed. He, too, as did all the 'great men' of the *Reich* that one knew of in recent times, took a typical 'ostrich policy', with his head buried in the sand, determined not to see the sorry end or admit the truth to himself a second sooner that was absolutely necessary. At heart that constituted a form of cowardice.

Göring's laughable over-estimation of the *Fallschirmjäger* divisions bordered on the grotesque. These divisions were, undoubtedly, good troops, but were still only human. Göring, however, thought they were supermen. One time he said in entire earnestness: "You must attack them with my two *Fallschirmjäger* divisions. Then you can chase the entire Russian army to the devil." Woe to him who spoke one single word against these troops. Göring took it as a personal insult.

Good as the *Fallschirmjäger* divisions might have been with respect to human material and equipment, they had great weaknesses in their middle and upper leadership. That was hardly surprising. How could one expect flying-officers – including proven and famous fighter and bomber pilots – suddenly brought to earth to effectively command battalions, regiments and divisions against so experienced an enemy as the Russians? Göring, however, zealously made sure that all of the ground-formations which were gradually emerging in increasing numbers from the no-longer flying *Luftwaffe* were composed exclusively of *Luftwaffe* personnel. This corresponded with his own vanity.

This is not the place to go into these serious mistakes that started with the activation of the so-called *Luftwaffenfelddivisionen* [*Luftwaffe* field divisions] in the fall of 1942. One thing, however, is certain – that this egotistical vanity of Göring's cost unending amounts of blood and had resulted in decisive defeats. It is widely known that Göring was a man who particularly loved external lustre, decorations and beautiful uniforms and there were many widespread jokes about this aspect of Hermann.

So it is, perhaps, revealing how he was dressed at that time when he visited us. Generally he wore an immense, extremely costly fur coat and a fur-cap with ear-flaps that made him look more like a genial old market-woman than a marshal. When he then removed his furs he had a 'special uniform' that was remarkable in that it was made of a pea-coat like thick, gray-green material similar to many articles of clothing that are, today, made from former military blankets. This uniform was not cut like the usual *Luftwaffe* uniform but was unique. Apparently this uniform was to have a 'simple field-uniform' effect. Upon it he wore only the great cross of the Iron Cross and the *Pour le Merite*. It is easily seen that the thick material of this uniform only made his massive figure more so. The giant, thick golden shoulder-straps were especially conspicuous. They were, undoubtedly, special issue, only for *Reichsmarschälle*.

When Göring had said enough about the military situation he often shifted into telling stories, without any proper transition. Thus I remember a long story from his time as a commercial pilot in Sweden. He was a really good, lively storyteller.

All in all, these visits only interfered with and caused significant difficulties for the *Heeresgruppe*. On his drives through the various localities Göring, like any high officer, ran into individual soldiers or elements of troops that, in his opinion, were less than fully disciplined and were loafing around. On every visit his *Ordonnanzoffizier* had to read us a report on these sinners. Göring then demanded sharp investigation and punishment of the responsible officers. We had much to do in investigating these things and the Commanders in Chief of the *Armeen* gradually developed a passionate hatred of the *Reichsmarschall*, who, apparently, had nothing better to do than see to the dress- and saluting- discipline in their rear areas. In a great many cases things turned out to be very different than how they were described. Thus, one time Göring was extremely outraged that, in Bad Freienwalde members of a replacement-troop unit there went to the movies in the afternoon with girls, while, at the front, other soldiers were in battle. Now, one can hardly prevent troops stationed in the actual homeland, when off-duty, from going to the movies and dating girls. Such complaints multiplied. Himmler always promised immediate and energetic action. He actually got upset that such things could happen in his *Heeresgruppe*. As he saw it, his name alone should prevent 'such misdeeds'.

It became really bad when Göring started to inspect rear positions. There he always determined that everything had to be made quite different, and, at last, one was tempted to ask him to give us a few sensible building instructions himself.

At the same time as the numerous visits by Göring came several visits by *Großadmiral* Dönitz. He came to discuss with Himmler the employment of the *Marine-Schützen-Division* [Naval Infantry Division]. Himmler had called on Dönitz to activate several divisions for employment on land from the large personnel reserves of the navy. These were then to be employed in the *Heeresgruppe 'Weichsel'* sector. In these new activations, Dönitz exhibited the same narrow-minded vanity as Göring had shown. His naval personnel would do it all on their own, and thus the first of these naval divisions came with an admiral as Division Commander and all the other officer positions right down to platoon leaders were likewise held by naval officers. The only army officer [*Heeresoffizier*] was the *Ia*, a young General Staff major. We learned from him that, here, again, the very best of human material and, for those bad times, a quite good level of equipment, was in danger of being ruined in a short time because of inexperienced and, for land warfare, poorly-trained officers. We had several experienced infantry officers evaluate the level of training of the division. The reports were uniformly devastating.

Finally a particularly competent *Heeres* division commander and a number of training officers and non-coms were employed with the division. Thanks to the excellent work of this commander, *Generalmajor* Bleckwenn, to the extent possible in the given time, this first *Marine-Schützen-Division* became a usable unit. It gave a good account of itself on the Oder Front south of Stettin. Activation of a second division was then initiated. As I remember, that was never fully completed since there was a lack of even the simplest items of equipment, especially weapons. There were not even enough rifles on hand to equip a division. That was what the German armaments industry had then come to in total war. I shall have to return to this sad chapter yet again.

I gained no convincing impression of *Großadmiral* Dönitz during his visits. He seemed to be no more than a mouthpiece of his *Führer*. The optimism he made such a show of could hardly be real. If, however, it actually was genuine, then one would have to ask how such an uncritical and not-especially clever man could be the actual Commander in Chief of the German *Kriegsmarine*. In naval circles Dönitz was nicknamed 'Hitlerjunge Quex'.[1] This nickname did, indeed, hit the nail on the head. Undoubtedly there was something fresh and youthful about him. That in itself could hardly qualify him for his position. This was the man whom Hitler appointed as his successor, shortly after he had handed over military and political command in the northern remnant of Germany.

Before I go into further military events involving *Heeresgruppe 'Weichsel'* I should highlight a few brief but illuminating experiences with several *Gauleiter*.

---

1   Translator's note – *Hitlerjunge* Quex was the protagonist of a novel and then a 1933 propaganda film based on the novel. A member of the Hitler Youth (*Hitlerjugend*), Herbert Norkus, nicknamed 'Quex', or 'Quicksilver', was killed while handing out Nazi flyers in a communist neighbourhood.

The first involves the *Gauleiter* of Posen, Greiser. He, too, had talked much of defending his *Gau* and, especially, its capital, to the last. However, before Posen was encircled, he showed up at the *Heeresgruppe*, sat around, unemployed, for a while and then wanted to become an *Ordonnanzoffizier*. There was much that this man could have been doing. He was, however, the picture of total helplessness, without any energy.

I frequently had to talk on the telephone with the *Gauleiter* of Mecklenburg, Hildebrandt. He had asked Himmler to give him daily orientation on the situation. I now had to do that. The main grounds for this interest appeared, judging from the questions he asked, his increasing anxiety over the approach of the Russians. There was hardly any trace of a material interest. He was horrified at every defeat and repeatedly broke into bitter reproaches regarding the troops and the military command. Repeatedly I refuted what he said quite bluntly. When he then, apparently, went on his way, we no longer needed to brief him.

One night I ran into three irresolute figures standing around in the central corridor of the barracks where my office was. A closer examination and questioning revealed that they were the *Gauleiter* of Brandenburg, Stürz, with his head of staff and adjutant. When I asked what they were doing there, Stürz said that he must speak to Himmler immediately. When asked why, he finally said that he wanted to be briefed on the situation.

I took the gentlemen into my little office and informed them that Himmler was not available at that time. Stürz then asked me to orient him. With the warning that I was not authorized to make any binding statements, I gave a general orientation, taking great care to keep the gentlemen away from the large situation map which they were exceedingly eager to devour. Here, too, they asked the same questions: "When will the Russians arrive?" "What do you believe can still be done?" Again, they showed nothing but pure anxiety in the face of the naked end. It was approaching 0600 hours in the morning and I was truly dead-tired and wanted to get at least one hour of sleep. The *Herr Gauleiter*, however, was oblivious. He wanted to chatter on and on about trivialities. When I could no longer keep my eyes open I excused myself.

Such kind of anxiety- and curiosity-driven visits constantly increased, since Himmler had a great number of party visitors. I refused to give that sort of orientation. First, I had a great deal to do, and then, I was not authorized for such. Indeed there was no way of knowing what use these great gentlemen would make of what they learned.

As the situation of *Heeresgruppe 'Weichsel'* became ever more unfavorable and more difficult, it became increasingly evident to Himmler that there were no more laurels there for him to earn. Doubtless he now realized that he was not competent for military command. Now he saw that his enemies, especially in the *Führer* headquarters, were making capital of these things. The open critics became ever more daring in personal attacks and there was good reason to believe that, behind them, at the head of the line was hiding his friend Martin Bormann, who wanted to finally get rid of this troublesome rival for influence with Hitler.

In addition Himmler was under constant pressure from the array of the highest *SS* commanders. They feared that they and the entire *SS* would also lose out if their *Reichsführer* lost power, so they continually importuned Himmler to lay down the problematical military command as soon as possible and get back into the immediate presence of Hitler to regain the influence that he had, in the meantime, lost. In this respect it must be recognized that, especially in the circles of the *Waffen-SS*, it was not just from purely egotistical arguments that this arose. Another reason was that, especially among the younger *SS* officers, there were many who still hoped that, with Himmler, if nothing else was possible, they would be able to set Germany on a new political course, particularly against the party *bonzes*.[2]

These men, inspired by upright and honorable intentions, found themselves making the same error as the men of 20 July 1944. Their somewhat vague but, undoubtedly, honorable intentions could no longer prevent the inevitable course of history that would bring the former Third *Reich* and Hitler to the approaching bitter end. Superficial judgements of 20 July simply said that it was 'too late'. I believe that both there and in regard to these intentions of the *Waffen-SS* it would be better to say: 'Impossible at an earlier time and therefore too late'.

One can and must charge Hitler and National Socialism with an unending list of crimes. That will, indeed, be done both abroad and also by ourselves. One thing, however, must be plainly established: This man came to power. He clearly achieved great success. He steered the entire world into one of the bloodiest wars ever and, apparently, nobody, either from outside or within, could prevent it. Thus, either Hitler was such a strong demonic force that neither the politicians of the other great powers acting from outside nor the forces of the opposition within Germany were strong enough to fetter him; or, on the other hand, the forces opposing Hitler internally and abroad delayed too long. If that was the case, this delay means that they must also shoulder a great share of the blame.

Looking at these things in retrospect as a very modest observer, the, perhaps, somewhat primitive thought comes to me that here the course of world history, for reasons incomprehensible to us ordinary little contemporaries, simply had to follow the course that it did. When history is written a hundred years from now clear relationships will certainly have become evident. But we will not be there to see it.

With his indecision Himmler now found himself in an evil predicament. On the one hand, under no circumstances did he want to ask his lord and master to relieve him of his command. On the other hand, he, naturally, did not want things to develop to a point where Hitler would remove him in a fit of anger. What, therefore, could he do? He hit upon the simple schoolboy wisdom of becoming ill as a way to escape his problems.

During these final days of Himmler with *Heeresgruppe 'Weichsel'* occurred the well-known attempt to enter into negotiations with the Western Powers through Sweden. I learned of this extremely secret attempt at that time from *SS Gruppenführer* von Alvensleben, then police-president of Dresden, whom I briefly knew. Alvensleben visited me one day (–? –)[3] in my office, behaved in a most secretive fashion – I had to send out a general staff officer who was present – and then informed me of the intention of persuading Himmler to open peace negotiations with the Western Powers through the Swedish Count Bernadotte. When asked for my humble opinion about such a highly political matter I offered only two points to consider:

2 Translator's note – *Bonze* was regularly employed as a derogatory term for the influential Nazi Party insiders who were close to Hitler and had his ear.
3 Translator's note – When the other missing dates were filled in from a 1957 memorandum from *Generalleutnant a.D.* Ferdinand Heim given above, this date remained unknown.

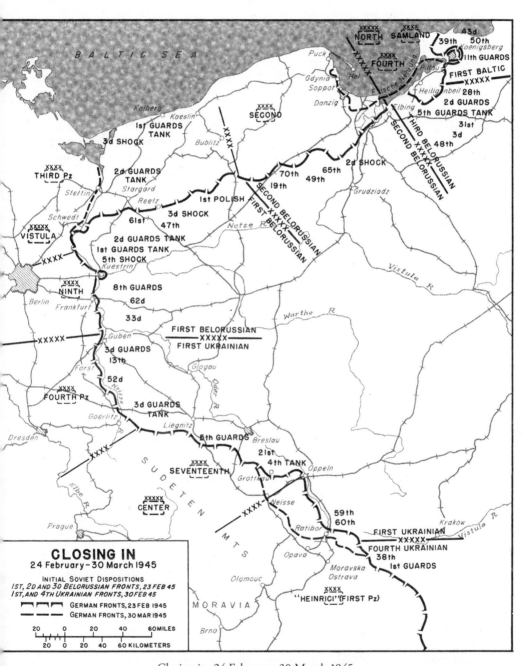

Closing in, 24 February–30 March 1945

1) I did not believe that, at the present time, one would be able to find anyone among the Western Powers who would be ready for negotiations;

2) It seemed to me that Himmler, in particular, was the most unsuitable man in all of Germany for such negotiations. That said, one might as well make the attempt. It certainly could not make the situation any worse. Alvensleben then had a long conversation with Himmler. He seemed quite pleased. After the fact I learned of the failure of this attempt.

The fighting on the *Heeresgruppe 'Weichsel'* front continued its unfavorable development. At that time (6 March 1945) its hotspot was with the 3rd *Panzerarmee* in the Stettin area. Kolberg was cut off and the battle for that historic city had begun. The 2nd *Armee* was engaged in heavy, bloody fighting in the Tucheler *Heide*[4] and for the last Vistula bridgeheads at Marienburg and Elbing. The fighting around Elbing, whose fate was particularly dear to me as my closest East Prussian homeland, was especially intense. The 2nd *Armee* put up its most bitter resistance on its southern front to maintain, for as long as possible, its freedom of movement south of the Baltic coast. However, it could neither prevent being forced back, step by step, to the north, nor could it prevent the Russians from turning its western flank. There the *Armee* attempted to occupy a thin line running generally from the Baltic near Stolpmünde – Stolp – west of Bütow ending approximately at the Brahe river. These security forces were unable anywhere to put up serious resistance on a front extending approximately 80 kilometers. Accordingly they had to limit their efforts to fight for the main intersections of the traffic routes. Essentially their assignment was to report in timely fashion to the *Armee* where the enemy was in this vacant area.

The lay person must be surprised at the rapid advance of the enemy in the area northwest of Danzig. On 12 March 1945 the Russians cut off the 2nd *Armee*. The end was clearly imminent and the *Heeresgruppe* had merely radio contact with this *Armee*. As noted above, the *Heeresgruppe* commanded the 2nd *Armee*, now, in name only. For some time the *Heeresgruppe* had no longer been able to provide help or have any influence on the course of events.

Although the current combat action was with the 3rd *Panzerarmee* and 2nd *Armee*, for a long time the attention of the command of the *Heeresgruppe* had been primarily focused on the 9th *Armee*. As mentioned above, a mighty storm was brewing against the 9th *Armee* sector. For weeks an extremely massive Russian concentration had been building astride the Warthe River. It was particularly notable for the concentration of strong armoured forces. The battle then raging in the area of Stettin was essentially related to this concentration.

Marshal Zhukov wanted to have the entire east bank of the Oder cleared of German forces for his great blow. A German bridgehead at Stettin would always constitute a certain threat to the flank. It was interesting to see how the Russian command, in spite of its massive successes at Posen, in West Prussia and Pomerania completed all preparations for the attack across the Oder against Berlin with painstaking exactitude. The reasons for that had to go beyond the well-known Russian caution. It appeared that the Russians wanted to again demonstrate to the world, and, not least, to their western

---

4   Translator's note – The Tucheler *Heide*, or heath, extended from just northeast of Könitz southeast nearly to Kulm, in West Prussia.

allies, the entire shattering weight of their mighty instrument of war and their strategic ability in a mighty military final apotheosis in their attack on the enemy capital. It would provide a steel exclamation point for the Yalta Conference, the brazen initial letter of the Potsdam Agreement and an impressive warning for later times. Finally it can be said that the battle of Berlin would draw the final double-line closing the accounts of the Russian reckoning at the Elbe.

In light of these massive Russian preparations, the *Heeresgruppe* requested additional forces to strengthen the Oder Front, especially for the 9th *Armee,* with ever increasing urgency. The *Heeresgruppe* reckoned that the enemy's main offensive would strike this *Armee* and would, indeed, be so massive that the front between Frankfurt and the Hohenzollern Canal would have to be uniformly strong and deeply held if immediate breakthroughs at several places were to be avoided. Adequate mobile reserves were also requisite behind the front of this *Armee,* for only with those could the inevitable Russian penetrations and bridgeheads be immediately smashed. The front of the 9th *Armee* extended about 120 kilometers.

The two 'fortresses' of Frankfurt and Küstrin were also on that front. They required strong additional forces for their defense. If such a front was to be defended with any hope of success against the main thrust of the enemy attack at least ten infantry divisions, with two additional infantry divisions for the two fortresses – a total of 14 infantry divisions – would be required in the front lines. Two armoured groups, each with two armoured divisions were needed as mobile reserve, the one in the area west of Frankfurt, the other in the area west of Küstrin. These rough calculations assume divisions at full authorized strength. If the divisions were weak and battered, the numbers would need to be raised by 25 – 30 %. There will certainly be many readers and also specialists who will laugh at all these theoretical ifs and buts, musts and ought-to's. However, this very example should clearly demonstrate that such practical calculations must form the foundation of military planning if one is to avoid losing the ground under his feet. A large part of the answer to the riddle, that was, in truth, no riddle, as to why the German front in the East was so often broken through and how the surprisingly rapid retreats came about lies in these dead numbers.

Bearing these demands in mind, the 9th *Armee* actually had at that time (mid-March) eight so-called infantry divisions in the front. In addition, the fortress-garrisons of Frankfurt and Küstrin – a motley collection of troops – consisted of approximately one-and-one-half weak infantry divisions in Frankfurt and a single weak infantry division in Küstrin. Of the eight front divisions of the *Armee,* only two, the 5th *Jägerdivision* and the 9th *Fallschirmjägerdivision,* could be said to correspond to divisions in their organization. The other six divisions were newly activated final-levée from training and reserve units, such as *Division 'Müncheberg',* the 169th *Division, Division 'Schlesien'* and the like. The 5th *Jägerdivision* had escaped from the 'Pomerania *Kessel* ' as remnants and was, originally, to have been reconstituted behind the front. Then, however, under the force of circumstances, it was again committed while it was in the midst of its reconstitution.

It can be determined that from a purely numerical viewpoint the infantry strength of the 9th *Armee* front was down nearly 50% from what was required. The deficiency in combat-worthiness cannot be expressed in numbers. It was, however, yet greater. The *Armee* had no mobile reserves at all available. It is, thus, understandable that the

Commander in Chief of the 9th *Armee, General der Infanterie* Busse, reported nearly daily in all clarity regarding the insupportable disproportion between the strength of our own troops and that to be expected of the enemy. This particular Commander in Chief was truly a man of unusual energy and competence, who also exhausted every possibility to make his decisive sector as capable of defense as could possible be done. It was amazing what makeshifts this *Armee* accomplished of every sort, especially in excellent construction of positions. All of that, however, could do nothing to make up for the lack of troops. Hitler and *OKH* had, as always, only empty rhetoric. There was talk of new activations, from which *Heeresgruppe 'Weichsel'* was then to receive something. We knew just what to expect of that kind of new activations.

Himmler, too, who was coming to see the complications ever more clearly, attempted on the basis of his position as Commander in Chief of the Replacement Army [*Oberbefehlshaber des Ersatzheeres*] to scrape up and activate everything possible. However, neither his Chief of Staff at the Replacement Army, Jüttner, nor his *Führungshauptamt* [high command headquarters] at the *SS* could come up with anything usable. The manpower was, in fact, still to be had, but no weapons and no matériel. If one examined the map of Greater Germany and determined how much of that remained in our hands, it would have to be obvious, even to any layman, that about 80% of the German armaments industry, already severely battered by the bombing attacks, had been lost, overrun by the enemy. Whence, then, were the actual weapons, equipment and matériel for newly activated units to come? There were no longer any stocks of weapons on hand. On one of his visits in March, Armaments Minister Speer happened to show me the list of all German armaments factories. Those which had been lost were crossed off in red. All that one saw on this list was red marks.

Thus in some fashion or another the attempt was made to remedy the lack of forces with ludicrous makeshifts. To replace the missing tanks, *Panzerjägerkommandos* [tank-hunting commandos] were formed. These were small troops of selected volunteers. Mounted on bicycles, they were armed with *Panzerfäuste* and machine pistols. Their mission was free-tank-hunting, especially against tanks that had broken through and at the lines of the anti-tank obstacles. In favorable terrain, in built-up localities and woods, they constituted an entirely credible enemy of armour. However, they were in no way a replacement for the missing armoured divisions.

Himmler was all afire with enthusiasm for these *Panzerjagdkommandos*, as he was for anything new and improvised. The staff officer for armour at the *Heeresgruppe*, *Oberst Freiherr* von Hauenschild, was entrusted with their activation. It was thanks to his unceasing initiative that *Heeresgruppe 'Weichsel'* activated a total of three so-called *Panzerjagdbrigaden*, including one composed of naval personnel. A particularly good foundation came from the so-called *Brigade 'Dirlewanger'* of the *Waffen-SS*.[5] It had been formed as a special unit composed of selected hunters and poachers and proved markedly effective.

Under pressure from Himmler a few battalions for infantry reinforcement were combed out of replacement units and the last units of the *Waffen-SS* and *Heer*. Arming them, however, raised significant difficulties.

---

5   Translator's note – The *Brigade 'Dirlewanger'* had become notorious for lawless behaviour and reprehensible excesses.

Within the context of these measures two units were sent to the 9th *Armee* that call for special mention. One was formed from the *Fahnenjunkerschule 'Wiener Neustadt'* [officer-candidate school *'Wiener Neustadt'*] and the other from the last remnants of the *Führungshauptamt* of the *Waffen-SS*, which was given the cover-name *'Tausendundeine Nacht'* [Thousand and One Nights]. Both regiments fought superbly to the very end. The *Fahnenjunkerregiment 'Wiener Neustadt'*, in particular, was, according to numerous eyewitnesses, a shining example of the best of what the German soldier could be. With an initial complement of about 1200 men, the regiment was almost completely wiped out. In recognition of their courage, the surviving members of the regiment were promoted, one-and-all, to *Leutnanten* in mid-April. That in itself is probably a unique occurrence in military history. However, this example also demonstrates how the very best of German blood, the cream of our youth, were being sacrificed at that time without rhyme or reason. The gaps these deaths tore in the ranks of our youth would be hard to heal in the future.

The *Reichsmarschall* and Dönitz made tremendous promises to Himmler. They would provide him with about 30-40,000 men, and as quickly as possible. The big question was simply with what were these men to be armed? These promises were never redeemed in Himmler's time. More shall be said about them later.

Part IX

In the desperate search for soldiers, Himmler suddenly got the idea of employing the so-called Russian *Wlassow-Division* [Vlasov Division] with *Heeresgruppe 'Weichsel'*. He requested this from Hitler. Hitler was, initially, opposed, as he had always been, to the formation of the so-called *'Wlassow-Truppe'*. Finally, however, in his dire need he agreed and Himmler was, again, inspired. We received the first information about this division from several officers of the *'Stabe für Osttruppen'* [Staff for Eastern Troops]. Since this attempt only took place after the departure of Himmler, its discussion will be postponed until later.

Himmler's 'cold' worsened steadily. In the meantime there was a change in the post of Chief of the General Staff of the *Heer* at *OKH*. *Generaloberst* Guderian left, as it was said, 'for reasons of health'. His successor was *General der Infanterie* Krebs, long-time Chief of the General Staff of *Heeresgruppe 'Mitte'* with *Feldmarschall* von Kluge, pre-war aide with the Military Attaché in Moscow. *General* Krebs brought a good reputation to his new position as Chief of the General Staff. He was known as a particularly clever man ˙and, above all, as a competent general staff officer, a man of many talents. Shortly after his appointment he made his courtesy visit to Himmler and oriented himself regarding the situation of the *Heeresgruppe*. The little, somewhat bow-legged man with glasses and an eternally friendly smile had something of a faun about him. He looked as if he loved the gentler pleasures of life. His conversation was marked with sparkling wit and a sharp spirit, generally a bit sarcastic. He was one of those chiefs of staff who always had a joke or an anecdote ready at the right time.

I was very surprised at the evaluation of the overall situation by this very clever officer who must have seen the actual situation precisely. He closely examined all of our concerns – and we had more of them than the hairs on our heads. As he described it problems came to usw there were, indeed, but these were already in the process of being solved. He briskly encouraged Himmler not to overestimate the Russians. *Heeresgruppe 'Schörner'* in Silesia had already achieved several notable successes. More would ensue and then the *Schwerpunkt* of the German defense could be shifted to *Heeresgruppe 'Weichsel'*. The most recent information that we received almost daily from our neighbour in the reciprocal situation-briefings, however, had a different sound. Except for a purely local success, the overall situation there was just as dark as ours. However, *OKH* generally liked to play off *Heeresgruppe 'Schörner'* against us. There, apparently, an entirely different attitude ruled. Its daily reports were far more confident than those of *'Weichsel'*. *Heeresgruppe 'Weichsel'* always saw the worst in everything. There was no faith in the final victory etc. In private, the new Chief of the General Staff used such words with me. I made a few factual and not even very humble objections. Thereupon he somewhat softened the criticisms while talking of the particularly horrible command relationships at the *Heeresgruppe*. I responded that, regardless of all else, I considered that the main difficulties lay in the disproportion between our forces and those of the Russians. To date, *OKH* had been unable to do anything to change that fundamental problem. In other respects, despite its better attitude, *Heeresgruppe 'Schörner'* had lost just as much in Silesia

72

General der Infanterie Hans Krebs, Chief of Staff of the *Heer*. (Bundesarchiv 146-1978-111-10A)

as we in Posen, West Prussia and Pomerania, even though they were far better situated strength-wise. Krebs disagreed with the last statement and opined that the Russians had placed their primary *Schwerpunkt* there. I responded only that, according to the latest enemy situation report that I had received from *OKH* the enemy concentration of forces facing *Heeresgruppe 'Weichsel'* was already greater than that facing *Heeresgruppe 'Schörner'* and was still increasing. Thus it came about that the farewell between Krebs and myself was rather rapid and chilly.

It was now clear to me what we could expect from this new Chief of the General Staff of the Army. Himmler was inspired by Krebs. He felt that finally we had a man who came to the difficult task with the necessary optimism, a man in whom the *Führer* would have the proper support; a better man, in any case, than the stubborn Guderian, who, in any case, with his poor health, was no longer really at his best. It was obvious that Himmler had learned nothing from his own bitter experience. It only required that someone make a few, pretty, encouraging remarks, as had *Herr* Krebs, and the situation was already rosy again. That, however, did not prevent Himmler from immediately becoming despondent in the afternoon of that very day on a visit to the Commander in Chief of the 9th *Armee*.

On this visit, *General* Busse presented all the concerns and difficulties that he must have in expectation of a soon-impending Russian offensive. The presentation was crystal clear and supported by large number of very relevant factual reports. Himmler was truly helpless in the face of these conclusive arguments. At the end he promised to personally

A command conference with Hitler at the HQ of Heeresgruppe 'Weichsel', early March 1945. Hitler is in conversation with (far right) *General der Infanterie* Theodor Busse, CO 9. *Armee*. (Bundesarchiv 146-1971-033-33).

present the whole situation yet again to Hitler. The only positive aid that he promised was the imminent commitment of the *Wlassow-Division* with the 9th *Armee*. *General* Busse was understandably rather disappointed.

At that time, roughly in mid-March, came an exciting event, Hitler's visit to the front of *Heeresgruppe 'Weichsel'*. This visit was, initially, kept completely secret. Even I only learned anything about it just before the event, and, then, only from a discussion of the security measures that would have to be taken by the *Heeresgruppe* and the 9th *Armee*. At the start there were some outlandish ideas. Apparently the roads that Hitler would follow on his approach were to be guarded by a sort of cordon of particularly reliable *SS* soldiers. That was, already, impossible in-and-of itself since it would have called for approximately one division for the stretch of about 50 kilometers. If one had that division, then it would hardly have been employed as a cordon, but would have been immediately committed in action. This great plan was soon discarded. The *Heeresgruppe* suggested no such street-guard but, instead, an extremely modest escort consisting of two to three inconspicuous vehicles with no particular markings, driving on back roads. Even Himmler was to drive separately to the rendezvous without escort. En route just *General* Busse, in whose *Armee* sector the visit was to take place, was to join and take over command. This proposal was then carried through and everything worked without mishap. From the *Heeresgruppe*, Himmler and the Chief of staff Lammerding attended. Details can, therefore, only be based on the accounts of eye- and ear- witnesses. The rendezvous was set at the headquarters of *Korps 'Berlin'* (so-named after *Kommandierende General der Artillerie* Berlin) on the northern wing of the 9th *Armee* at the Oder River northwest of Küstrin, in an old manor house of *Feldmarschall Fürst* [Prince] Blücher von Wahlstatt in Neuhardenberg.[1]

A number of division and regimental commanders of the 9th *Armee* were ordered to that site with no advance knowledge of who was awaiting them there. Hitler was said to have made an extremely weary, sickly impression. In contrast to his accustomed behaviour, he hardly said a word. He listened to the situation briefing of the Commander in Chief of the 9th *Armee* and several individual reports by various commanders. It was said that all concerned were, unanimously, extremely uncompromising regarding the great weakness of this vital front. The entire affair lasted about one-and-a-half hours, after which Hitler drove back to Berlin, never again to leave his *'Malepartus'*[2], the bunker in the *Reichskanzlei*, before his death. Hitler had, however, made a promise to the Commander in Chief of the 9th *Armee*, namely, as soon as possible to send several armoured forces as mobile reserve. Inquiry to *OKH* drew the response: "As soon as the

---

1   Translator's note – *Feldmarschall* Gebhard Leberecht von Blücher (1742–1819) was a hero of the German War of Independence from Napoleon, noted for bold, aggressive, effective action. He is still known in Germany as *Marschall Vorwärts*, 'Marshal Forwards'. As a Prussian *Graf* (Count), later elevated to *Fürst* [Prince] *von Wahlstatt*, he led Prussian troops against Napoleon, most memorably at Waterloo, where his troops arrived at a critical moment and broke the enemy right flank. The term, *'Wahlstatt'* is a rather poetical term meaning 'battlefield', so, as *'Fürst von Wahlstatt'*, Blücher was given the title 'Prince of the Battlefield'.

2   Translator's note – Here Eismann is referring to a character from folklore that sprang to popularity when Johann Christoph Gottsched published *Reynard the Fox* in German in 1752, the story later being edited and further popularised by Goethe in 1794. Malepartus, who reappears in literature after the 18th Century, takes the form of a bad or evil creature who inhabits a lair, retreating back there after his misdeeds.

General der Infanterie Eberhard Kinzel, Chief of Staff of *Heeresgruppe 'Weichsel'*
21 March-22 April 1945. (Bundesarchiv 146-1985-048-28)

situation of *Heeresgruppe 'Schörner'* permits, the promised reserves will come from there." That was a rather vague promise, regarding which *General* Busse was not very happy when I shared it with him.

A short time after this great event Himmler went to bed and we were told that he had dangerous angina.

The command of the *Heeresgruppe* became yet more difficult, since the great Lord Himmler now required great tenderness and discussions mainly took place at his sickbed. His personal physician was always present. Hardly a loud word was uttered. In brief, he put on quite a performance.

A few days after Himmler had taken to his bed, about 2 March 1945, the door of my office opened and, to my great surprise, there stood *Generalleutnant* Kinzel before me, whom I had known as a division commander in extremely heavy fighting on the Tucheler *Heide*.

After a heartfelt greeting – he had been general staff officer of my peacetime division in Hannover – he explained to me that he had been ordered, with immediate effect, by order of *OKH* to *Heeresgruppe 'Weichsel'*. Everything moved so fast that he had not yet even had time to turn the command of his division over to his successor. Within a few hours of the *OKH* order he was already starting for here from the Danzig airfield. He asked me if I knew what he was supposed to do here.

I knew nothing of his appointment. Accordingly I suggested that he should report, as soon as possible, to Himmler. Perhaps he could answer this riddle. The report arrived later that day and then we, meaning Lammerding and I, were finally told by *General* Kinzel what his sudden appearance signified. Once again it had to do with an entirely new invention of Hitler's and *OKH* in the area of military command.

Generalleutnant Kinzel was to function as sort of a second *Heeresgruppe* Chief of General Staff to support the 'sick' Himmler. In normal times in such a situation either the senior *Armee* Commander in Chief would be appointed as the sick commander's deputy, or, for a longer period, a new Commander in Chief would be named. With this, however, we now had two chiefs of general staff, one from the *Heer* and the other from the *Waffen-SS*. The question now was simply, which of the two would officiate, *Generalleutnant* Kinzel or *Gruppenführer* Lammerding? (Lammerding had been promoted in March to *Gruppenführer und Generalleutnant der Waffen-SS*.) *OKH* had adroitly avoided giving any directives regarding this. *Generalleutnant* Kinzel opined that he would let the matter rest, initially, and then a solution would develop of itself. The choice of *Generalleutnant* Kinzel for this difficult and vital function seemed both to him and to me extremely remarkable, since Kinzel was actually by no means a favorite of Hitler nor of his clique.

At the start of the war *Oberst i.G.* Kinzel was the chief of *Abteilung 'Fremde Heere Ost'* [Enemy Army Intelligence East] in the General Staff of the *Heer*. Thus he was the authority responsible for all questions about the East and, above all, for the evaluation of the Russian armed forces. Shortly before the start of the Eastern Campaign he had suddenly been relieved. It was rumoured that, at that time, he had already offended Hitler. I now learned from Kinzel himself what the reason had been. In all the armies of the world the general staffs put together and kept current figures of the strength, armament, equipment and organization of adjoining armies and, above all, of potential enemies. These figures, so vital to war, were, from the start, published in more-or-less comprehensive books and then issued to the commands and troops to put them in the picture regarding the enemy and his strength. Kinzel had to present one of these 'Red Books', as we called it, to the Chief of the General Staff and to Hitler, shortly before the Eastern Campaign.

Hitler read it and then disapproved it, with the remark that it was exaggerated and painted far too black a picture of the military strength of Russia, which he did not believe. Such a thing could not be given to the troops. It would only frighten them. He demanded the immediate production of a suitably milder version, more favorable to us.

Accordingly, thousands of copies of the book that had already been prepared, soberly factual and, so far as generally known, correct in its statistics, had to be destroyed. The replacement version of the 'Red Book' on the Russian armed forces was completely inadequate. It had to provide figures on the strength and armament of the Red Army with the fully recognized intention of encouraging the German troops and commands. That was turning the methods of Goebbels' propaganda to serious military matters. Kinzel resisted such a knowing falsification and had to go.

The same held true for the then-military attaché in Moscow, *General* Köstring. He was, undoubtedly, one of the best experts on the Russian army. When, after his return from Moscow, he wanted to report to Hitler regarding the actual strength of Russia, Hitler would not hear any of it, dismissing him with a wave of his hand, and *General* Köstring vanished into a trivial post in oblivion. Hitler did not want to hear the truth about his new opponent.

Oberst Kinzel was then employed in the general staff of the *Truppe* [arm or branch of service] and had so proven himself as a *Korps-* and *Armee-* chief of general staff that he finally became Chief of the General Staff of *Heeresgruppe 'Nord'*. There another set-to developed with Hitler regarding the conduct of the war in Kurland. Kinzel and his Commander in Chief, *Generaloberst* Lindemann, expressed the opinion that Kurland should be evacuated punctually and the Kurland forces employed in a more important location. He and his Commander in Chief were yanked out of there. He received a *Volksgrenadier Division* in the 2nd *Armee*.

After the background outlined above, it seems remarkable that this was the man who had been selected to advise Himmler. It is possible that Himmler himself, who had come to know *General* Kinzel as a division commander, requested him. Whatever the grounds for his appointment it was quite clear that neither we nor *General* Kinzel could alter the situation.

Aside from the unclear command relationships as to who, now, was the actual, functioning chief of the general staff, I was personally extremely pleased with the presence of *Generalleutnant* Kinzel, for now I finally had a superior who actually understood something about the command of a *Heeresgruppe* and with whom one could work for the good of the whole. After *Generalleutnant* Kinzel had me brief him in a long discussion regarding the current situation of the *Heeresgruppe*, but also over what had led up to it, he shook his head again and again in incomprehension, even though he, too, had his own full measure of bitter experiences in this war. This excellent soldier was still so much in his previous position as division commander in the heavy fighting of his division in West Prussia that he needed some time to grasp the true context and the complete untenability of the military situation. This must be seen as an especially good and striking example of how difficult it was for the troop commanders, even if they were experienced general staff officers, to gain a more-or-less clear picture of the big picture, to say nothing of the simple man at the front.

Generalleutnant Kinzel finally asked me for an evaluation of the situation. It ran, in brief, as follows:

The 2nd *Armee* was approaching its demise in West Prussia unless there was an immediate decision to, at least, withdraw strong elements of it by sea. That, however, was not to be expected in light of Hitler's determination, to date, to act as he had with regard to East Prussia and Kurland. In fact, the more the army was compressed, the more enemy forces were freed up for his operation against the Oder. The Oder Front of the *Heeresgruppe* was extremely inadequately manned. On paper, the 9th *Armee* front appeared to be more-or-less defensible. A closer examination of the actual forces, however, revealed that, in detail, it was actually weak. In its present condition, without reserves, this *Armee* was not in a position to successfully deal with Russian penetrations at several locations. The 3rd *Panzerarmee* was an *Armee* in name only. Its only troops that had any combat worthiness were fighting at the time with extraordinarily heavy daily losses at the Stettin bridgehead. The Oder sector of this *Armee*, extending about 50 kilometers, could only be said to be watched, but neither held nor defended. The troops committed there – a naval *Volkssturm*[3] and a Ukrainian SS battalion – had very limited combat-worthiness. As for artillery, there was practically nothing, aside from a few, largely immobile, *Flak* guns. Reserves were just as limited here as with the 9th *Armee*. Command relationships in this Oder sector were inadequate. Despite the Oder barrier, an attack against this sector would be a walkover for the enemy. At the time the Russians did not, indeed, appear to intend an attack here. That, however, could change daily. On the other side, the enemy picture was roughly as follows:

About eight to ten Russian infantry armies faced the 9th *Armee*. Behind them were armoured forces consisting of two, possibly three, tank armies whose current concentration *Schwerpunkt* was in the area north of Küstrin. In the battle for Stettin the 3rd *Panzerarmee* was under attack by about four to five infantry armies and about two tank armies. It is likely that one of these two tank armies had been drawn out of this mass of armour by the armour of the 9th *Armee*. Facing the Oder Front of the 3rd *Panzerarmee* was yet another infantry army on a broad front. All in all, facing *Heeresgruppe* 'Weichsel' – less the 2nd *Armee* – were 14 –15 Russian infantry armies and four to five tank armies.

The Russian intention was clear and simple: Breakthrough to Berlin on both sides of Küstrin, presumably within ten days at most, so far as could be seen from the state of preparations for the attack.

General Kinzel fully endorsed this evaluation.

The previous and, nominally, still functioning Chief of the General Staff, SS *Gruppenführer* Lammerding, quickly withdrew himself from the business. He acted like a man who felt himself freed from a bad nightmare. He really revived. In the meantime, Himmler's cold so worsened that he had to go to his friend Gebhardt in Hohenlychen.

---

3   Translator's note – The original manuscript uses the term *Marinevolkssturm*. Since this does not appear to relate to a type of unit hitherto encountered the author may have been referring simply to a *Volkssturm* unit, or possibly a mixed alarm unit built from *Kriegsmarine* and *Volkssturm* elements.

Generaloberst Gotthard Heinrici (right), commander of *Heeresgruppe 'Weichsel'*
21 March-29 April 1945. This image was taken in September 1943, when
Heinrici was CO 4. *Armee*. (Bundesarchiv 146-1977-120-09)

There he could only rarely be disturbed. He did, however, remain officially in command of the *Heeresgruppe*. In actual fact there was no longer a Commander in Chief available. Accordingly, *General* Kinzel practically commanded the *Heeresgruppe*. This circumstance greatly increased the *Ia's* workload. Finally, in the last days of March, Hitler decided to recall Himmler for reasons of health. *Generaloberst* Heinrici, formerly Commander in Chief of the 4th *Armee*[4] was appointed as his successor. On 20 March 1945 he replaced Heinrich Himmler in command of *Heeresgruppe 'Weichsel'*. In great haste the 'Field Command Post of the *Reichsführer-SS*' packed up and pulled out. Himmler, who suddenly regained his health upon being recalled, did not miss the opportunity to celebrate a magnificent turnover of his command to his successor. For this the command section of the *Heeresgruppe* had to prepare all map records and important orders since its activation for a major report. Although there was much real work to be done, this purely

---

4   Translator's note – *Oberst* Eismann is in error. *Generaloberst* Gotthard Heinrici did, indeed, command the 4th *Armee*, but that was earlier in the war, in 1942. Sent to a 'convalescent home' in Karlsbad in 1943 as punishment for refusing to burn Smolensk in accord with the Nazi scorched earth policy, Heinrici was recalled to service in the summer of 1944 and assigned command of the German 1st *Panzerarmee* and attached Hungarian 1st Army, during which command he fought with consummate skill and determination. He was awarded the *Schwerten zum Ritterkreuz mit Eichenlauben* [Swords to the Oak Leaves of his Knight's Cross] on 3 March 1945.

military historical work had to be prepared with priority, so that Himmler could present his successor with a report of his former heroic deeds.

I was present at this occasion, which might have been called Himmler's 'accounting'. Sitting in the midst of mountains of situation maps and other papers, Himmler held forth to *Generaloberst* Heinrici about his military career for, I believe, three hours. Here, for the last time, the pure layman held the spotlight. The most inconsequential things were presented in great detail. After three hours nobody knew what this actually related to. It was shocking, and had that effect on the new Commander in Chief. To this man, especially, such a totally theatrical military swan-song, untroubled by any factual knowledge, in a military situation that was more than serious, was deeply astonishing, indeed, downright disgusting.

Generaloberst Heinrici was, for us, the archetype of an old Prussian officer. When one saw this serious, taciturn, erect little general with his natural courtesy listening to the lengthy report of the absolutely unsoldierly, excitedly gesturing Himmler, one recognized that two worlds were facing each other. During the brief and difficult time that I had the good fortune to serve under *Generaloberst* Heinrici, I learned to honor and respect him to the highest possible degree. He certainly did not belong to those conspicuous, glittering and, at times, inspired military leaders of which, even in the Second World War, Germany possessed an entire series – or, better put, had possessed, for most had been sent packing by Hitler.

Generaloberst Heinrici was far more the soldier grown gray in long service who had constantly gone his way in tough, iron-hard work. On his path he had held practically all the positions of military command, both as a leader of troops and also as a general staff officer. Thus, in him, great practical experience and great military knowledge complemented each other to the highest degree.

Part X

This man was not exactly inspired by the inheritance he was walking into. Even though the situation of his 1st *Armee* with attached Hungarian 1st Army, in Hungary, had not been particularly favorable, he found far more difficult conditions here with the *Heeresgruppe*. Even Himmler's grandiloquent speech could not conceal that.

In contrast to Himmler, he immediately visited the armies that were under his command. A visit to the 2nd *Armee* by flying to Danzig was no longer feasible. In the meantime there had been a change in the command of the 3rd *Panzerarmee*. *Generaloberst* Raus had been replaced by *General der Panzertruppen* von Manteuffel, holder of the *Ritterkreuz mit Schwertern und Brillanten* [Knight's Cross with Swords and Diamonds]. Whether this change was necessary remains an open question. In any case, the 3rd *Panzerarmee* received a fine leader in *General* von Manteuffel, whose superlative qualities as commander of armoured formations could no longer be utilized. Indeed, this *Panzerarmee* had, in effect, only one, single, *Panzerdivision*. Cooperation between the *Heeresgruppe* and the command of this *Armee* was good. I knew its Chief of General Staff, *Generalmajor* Müller-Hillebrandt, from previous service and its First General Staff Officer [*Ia*] *Oberst i.G.* Ludendorff – nephew of *General* Ludendorff – was of the same age-class as me.

The new Commander in Chief returned from this first visit to the *Armee* with deep concern. Both *Armee* commanders had given him an unvarnished account of their difficulties. Thus, the picture that he had already gained from the staff of the *Heeresgruppe* had been rounded out with a great number of important details.

In the 9th *Armee* sector the Russians had gradually strengthened their reconnaissance thrusts over the Oder. These had now transitioned to local attacks with extremely effective artillery preparation. These individual, narrowly limited attacks, repeatedly shifting to different places on the Oder Front finally resulted in the enemy having a strong foothold and initial small bridgeheads on the west bank. He built the first bridgeheads of this sort between Frankfurt and Küstrin at Reitwein and Lebus. Soon afterward, however, the enemy was also firmly established on the west bank of the Oder northwest of Küstrin at Questebiese. It was particularly difficult for the defender to eliminate these bridgeheads because the Russians attacked simultaneously at so many places. Thanks to the lack of local reserves there were generally insufficient forces in our counterattacks to force the enemy back over the river. During the night-time hours the enemy brought over considerable reinforcements, especially heavy weapons, very early. These were primarily mortars, but he also brought over individual guns. Thus these initial little ulcers ate their way deeper into our front. As the next step the Russians then set about uniting two adjoining small bridgeheads to thereby build a larger bridgehead with a significantly broader base.

With these tactics the enemy would clearly succeed in a few days in building the requisite jump-off positions on both sides of Küstrin for his armoured forces on the west bank of the Oder. As a start to this bitter and eventful battle the Russians succeeded

General der Panzertruppe Hasso von Manteuffel, CO 3. *Panzerarmee*
from March 1945. (Bundesarchiv 146-1978-111-10A)

in taking Küstriner Neustadt, the part of Küstrin on the west bank of the Oder, pretty much by surprise. The commander of the position, *SS Gruppenführer* Rheinefarth[1], was relieved by Himmler for this and was to have been court-martialled. At Frankfurt, on the other hand, a German bridgehead was still held on the east bank of the Oder.

It was clear to *OKH*, to the *Heeresgruppe*, to the 9th *Armee,* indeed, through the *Korps* right down to the company commanders in the front lines, that these Russian bridgeheads constituted a deadly menace. There was no room for doubt that the troops at the front had done all that they possibly could to immediately hurl the Russians back wherever they had crossed the Oder. The troops, however, were too weak. The divisions had no reserves at all. The *Korps*, the *Armeen* and the *Heeresgruppe* reserves were so minimal that they were never quite able to achieve success. Every counterattack, however, caused yet more attrition. It was easy to see that the limited reserves would be expended in these tactics and even to set a time when this would take place, and it would be before the actual Russian attack had even begun. There is a basic military maxim that if an enemy landing on a coast or on the bank of a river is not smashed at the very beginning by concentrating all forces, then it never will be smashed. This had already proved itself in the invasion in the West. Here it was precisely the same on a small scale.

OKH was incapable of providing the *Heeresgruppe* with even the relatively limited reserves required to enable the 9th *Armee* to eliminate these initially weak enemy bridgeheads. By the time a decision was finally made to provide some armoured forces it was too late. With these first needle-pricks the Russians killed two flies with one blow. First, they built the springboard for the attack on Berlin. Second, they eroded the already slim forces defending the German front before the start of their attack, at the very least significantly weakening them.

Hitler and *OKH* raged at the daily reports that, despite extreme efforts of the troops and constantly increasing friendly losses, it remained impossible to force the enemy back over the Oder. The *Heeresgruppe* could not change it. Hitler now got the idea of repeatedly destroying the Russian crossings – there were already a whole number of bridges under construction – to, at least, stop the supply of troops and matériel. Two special technical combat measures were to be employed to accomplish this: a *Stuka Staffel* under command of the famous *Oberstleutnant* Baumbach and a special *Abteilung* of the *Kriegsmarine* with so-called *'Kleinkampfmitteln'* [guerilla tactics].

The *Sonderstaffel* [special squadron] – it consisted of the only friendly aircraft that still flew in our area – was to destroy the Russian bridges from the air with special radio-guided bombs. The *Kriegsmarine* was to attack the bridges from the water with small, explosive-laden, radio-directed boats. The results of both were minimal. The Russians protected against aerial attack with their far-superior air forces and correspondingly strong anti-aircraft guns. The explosive-laden boats were fended off by simple timber-barriers in front of the bridges.

Right after the first attempts *Oberstleutnant* Baumbach explained to me that any further attacks by his *Staffel* would be pointless. If the bridges – generally only one or another of six or seven – were hit, they were repaired within a few hours. Losses of our aircraft were totally out of proportion to the results, and the same could be said regarding the expenditure of the fuel that had become so precious. It is hardly believable, but it was true, that the flights of this single *Staffel* used up most of the aviation gasoline that remained to us. *Oberstleutnant* Baumbach finally stated that it would be better to let a few fighters take off with his fuel, even if it provided no real help, to at least give the troops at the front a little reassurance.

In *Oberstleutnant* Baumbach I also got to know one of those good types of our fliers who was famous for his great successes. Despite his high decorations and his undoubted great successes he had nothing of the *prima donna* about him that one often finds, especially among fighter pilots. Simple, modest, yet self-confident, as justified by his great successes, from him I learned a great many revealing particulars about the reasons for the downfall of our *Luftwaffe*. He, too, had to place the primary blame on his Commander in Chief, Göring, who, despite timely and ever-repeated suggestions from his commanders and officers disregarded all sound advice and let this vital weapon deteriorate.

In the 3rd *Panzerarmee* sector the battle for Stettin approached its end during the time from 15 to 19 March. The massed, concentric Russian attack from the south, east and north had reduced our bridgehead from its initial extent, from north of Greifenhagen on the Oder – east of Altdamm – Gollnow – Stepenitz at the Stettiner *Haff* to the narrow area around Altdamm. The northern part around Gollnow had been lost extremely quickly. There the *Armee* had only been able to commit weak elements of the garrison of Stettin, consisting essentially of remnants of X *SS Korps*. III *SS Panzerkorps* with the 10th *SS Panzerdivision 'Frundsberg'*, the remnants of *Divisionen 'Nordland'* and *'Nederland'* and the 5th *Fallschirmjägerdivision*. These troops had fought superbly in incessant long days of heavy fighting and exacted very heavy bloody losses from the Russians. Nevertheless, they could not prevent the final loss of what had become a senseless bridgehead. With great difficulty the *Heeresgruppe* convinced Hitler and *OKH* to grant permission at the last moment to evacuate the futile remnant of the bridgehead. Thus at least a portion of the best troops of the 3rd *Panzerarmee*, who were urgently needed for defense of the Oder Front, were saved before the final collapse.

At about the same time, 4–17 March, the battle of Kolberg took place. The defense of this 'fortress' for a limited time made sense in that a great number of refugees from the East, particularly from East and West Prussia, had sought refuge there from the Russians. These unfortunates and the bulk of the population of the city itself could still be saved from the Russians by sea. That long, but not one day longer, must the city be defended. *Oberst* Fullriede was named Commandant of this 'fortress' after its encirclement. This *Oberst*, an old Southwest Africa man, had actually been transferred as a division commander from the Italian Front to the *Heeresgruppe*. Since it had not yet been decided where to employ him, the *Heeresgruppe* had sent him to examine the situation at Kolberg. He arrived in Kolberg just in time to be cut off there. Since the Kolberg Commandant at that time – I have forgotten his name – was not considered up to this difficult task, *Oberst* Fullriede was made Fortress Commandant on the spot.

This would turn out to be an ideal solution. It was only thanks to the indefatigable initiative, energy and personal courage of this officer that the wholly inadequately garrisoned city put up such tough resistance against manifoldly superior Russian forces and that it was possible to evacuate the entire civilian population of Kolberg by sea. Approximately 40-50,000 people, especially women and children, owe their lives to the courageous defenders, and, above all, their Commandant, who fought almost to the last man.

As the last of the civilian population were evacuated, *Oberst* Fullriede and the sorry remnants of his garrison – about 200 men – were so compressed into the harbour quarter of the city that these men fought a purposeless and hopeless battle with their backs literally directly at the water. *Oberst* Fullriede radioed to the 3rd *Panzerarmee* a request that he and his remaining men embark on a destroyer that had supported the battle from the sea. Thereupon the Commander in Chief of the 3rd *Panzerarmee*, *General* von Manteuffel, immediately called *Generaloberst* Heinrici and requested permission from the *Heeresgruppe*. Because it involved a fortress that would thus be evacuated, the *Heeresgruppe* had to request this permission from Hitler. He, as always, refused. In the meantime a direct radio message arrived at the *Heeresgruppe* from Kolberg with the same request. *Generaloberst* Heinrici was outraged over the senseless sacrifice of these brave men. *Generaloberst* Heinrici had a radio message sent to the Commandant of Kolberg that had to be extremely carefully phrased so that *OKH* and, with it, Hitler, who listened in on the *Heeresgruppe* radio traffic, would not again interfere.

The radio message permitted Fullriede to embark. For Fullriede this had taken too long, and he had good reason. He suddenly radioed the laconic message: 'After bitter fighting I and the remainder of the garrison have embarked on the destroyer.' At both 3rd *Panzerarmee* and at the *Heeresgruppe* there was great concern as to how Hitler would react to this independent decision of Fullriede. Unquestionably it had been overheard. *Generaloberst* Heinrici immediately said that he would cover for Fullriede, no matter what happened. It was said that, in any case, Fullriede would get something around his neck.[2] Either the *Eichenlaub* or the noose. I pass on these not entirely tasteful words only because they best describe the actual situation. *Oberst* Fullriede and his faithful few made it safely to Swinemunde and were received by the 3rd *Panzerarmee* with full honors.[3] He reported to the *Heeresgruppe* the next day. His straightforward report of the battle of Kolberg and of the suffering of the civilian population during the final difficult days was deeply moving. Fullriede lauded their conduct as beyond all praise. He was ordered to see Hitler the next day and returned without the noose and with the well-earned *Eichenlaub zum Ritterkreuz*. Apparently Hitler must have had a good day.

Following the loss of the Stettin bridgehead, large-scale enemy regrouping on the Oder Front of the 3rd *Panzerarmee* indicated that the Russian offensive over the Oder was immediately impending.

One small episode bears repeating. A small bridgehead was held at Schwedt to permit reconnaissance in the extremely dubious area southwest of Pyritz. The Commandant of this bridgehead was *SS Obersturmbannführer* Skorzeny, recently known for his acquittal in a war-crimes trial and his liberation of Mussolini. He defended the bridgehead with two battalions and conducted extremely successful reconnaissance operations. The Russians decided rather suddenly to eliminate this constant source of irritation, attacking with

2   Translator's note – The *Ritterkreuz* and *Eichenlaub* (Knight's Cross and Oakleaves thereto) were worn on a ribbon around the neck, the alternative, of course, being the hangman's noose.
3   Translator's note – Swinemunde is the port where the Stettiner *Haff* exits to the Baltic Sea (*Ostsee*) through the Swine. The term '*Haff*' is used for the large coastal lagoons behind coastal sand spits and sand bars along the Baltic Sea, such as the Frisches *Haff* and Stettiner *Haff*.

increasingly strong forces. The *Heeresgruppe* wanted to evacuate the bridgehead, which had become useless. The first-class *SS* battalions were urgently needed behind the Oder for defense. Hitler forbade the withdrawal. Since bridges were no longer available, only ferries, the decision for evacuation had to be made promptly. Because of Hitler's refusal, the main body of the two battalions was destroyed. Skorceny and the miserable remnants were forced to swim the river under heavy enemy fire, during which yet another large number of soldiers drowned.

The *Heeresgruppe* had already made repeated requests that the unfortunate 2nd *Armee* be controlled directly by *OKH*. As already explained, the *Heeresgruppe* could neither help nor effectively command this *Armee* after its encirclement. In this instance, and more than on the rest of its front, the *Heeresgruppe* had sunk to doing no more than passing along Hitler's orders.

The 2nd *Armee* fought its hopeless battle with great tenacity. It had, in the meantime, been compressed into a narrow bridgehead (better put, beachhead) of Gotenhafen/ Danzig. Hotly contested Elbing was lost in especially heavy and bloody fighting. There the 7th *Panzerdivision*, true to its old reputation, fought splendidly for yet another, final time. Hitler did, finally, accept the *Heeresgruppe* request and, on 13 March, *OKH* took direct command over the 2nd *Armee*. The *Heeresgruppe's* farewell radio message to that *Armee* left me with a renewed feeling of deep shame that the *Heeresgruppe* had failed in saving the *Armee* from this senseless destruction.

Minimal remnants evacuated by sea to the *Heeresgruppe*. That involved VII *Panzerkorps* with a few fragments of troops. From these men we learned more of the bitter fighting in Danzig, itself, which had nearly totally destroyed that beautiful old Hanseatic city with its famous architecture.

The more threatening the situation at the Oder became for the 9th *Armee*, the more urgent were its demands to the *Heeresgruppe* for the immediate provision of additional forces. *Generaloberst* Heinrici, who telephoned *General* Krebs almost every day, never failed to present this vital question in all its urgency. Aside from lectures and unfounded promises that probably were never conceived of as anything more than consolation, he received nothing. One day a general staff officer of the *'Stab für Ostruppen'* [Staff for Eastern Troops] reported to us. He wanted to discuss the commitment of the *'Wlassow – Division'* [Vlasov Division]. His statements made clear that the division would be available at any time. It was training at a troop training ground in southern Germany. Its armament and equipment were that of a normal German infantry division. After discussion with the Commander in Chief, it was agreed with the general staff officer that *General* Wlassow, himself, would come as soon as possible for a conference at the *Heeresgruppe*. The commitment of this division, which had been planned back in Himmler's time, had already caused general headaches at that time.

Even though the responsible *'Stab für Osttruppen'* had rendered judgement that the division was reliable and ready for immediate employment at any time we still had serious reservations. We just could not accept the idea that a Russian volunteer division, all of whose officers, including the division commander, were also Russian, could be expected now, at the last minute, to fight effectively against their own fellow countrymen. The total defeat of Germany was too obvious for these Russians to fail to draw quite rational conclusions about their own fate. Here was another of the missed opportunities of which there were so many similar examples in this war.

Back when we conquered the Ukraine we were met by a sincere wave of enthusiasm. The German soldier was celebrated as the liberator from the Bolshevist yoke. The Ukrainian prisoners of war believed that their hour had come, and hoped to be employed immediately in the war against Bolshevism. Several German commanders in chief, including *Feldmarschall* von Bock, suggested to Hitler that the Ukraine should be granted its independence under German sovereignty and a Ukrainian Liberation Army be formed.

This proposal would have brought us an initially content, perhaps even grateful, Ukraine and about one million usable soldiers. Hitler, however, harshly rejected this sensible proposal. His head was filled with supermen and slave-peoples. He turned over future *Ostpolitik* [Eastern politics] to his *Ostminister* Rosenberg and set up all his satrap men, such as *Ostgauleiter* Koch, over the Ukraine.

The result was soon overwhelming. Resentment and hatred against the new oppressor gradually dispelled the hate against Bolshevism. This resentful population then became the decisive support for the ever-strengthening Russian partisan movement in all parts of occupied Russia. This narrow-minded, arrogant stupidity and awkwardness in handling foreign peoples was most conspicuous, to me, in Yugoslavia. Even in France, where we wanted to achieve peaceful cooperation as soon as possible, yes, even with our own allies, such as Rumania and Hungary, at every turn one ran into completely irrational and stupid measures. What the German soldier had won almost everywhere in Europe, at least by way of respect, the politicians then transformed in the briefest of time into its opposite.

The Wlassow Division was to be employed with the 9th *Armee*. *General* Busse, who was fundamentally opposed to employment of the Russians, wanted to present a proposal as to how the Wlassow Division could be brought into experimental commitment without disadvantage to our own situation. Further employment of this division would be made dependant on the success of this action. The simplest approach would have been to employ the division in an, at that time, still quiet sector of the 3rd *Panzerarmee*. There it could cause the least harm. However, apparently these Russians also had their own special pride. They insisted that, at the least, they should be used solely as attack troops.

General Wlassow came to us at the beginning of April, accompanied by his Russian adjutants, a German general staff officer and an interpreter. Wlassow was a big, somewhat gaunt man. His features were coarse, as if hewn from wood. He had extremely lively, clever eyes, a somewhat pale complexion and, although faultlessly shaven, the sort of bluish shimmer that dark-haired men often have. His mighty, broad, somewhat forward-arched forehead was conspicuous, meeting a large bald spot. He wore a simple fantasy-uniform of Russian cut. He did understand some German but conversed with us in Russian through the interpreter.

After the initial courtesies, *Generaloberst* Heinrici immediately got to the heart of the matter. He openly asked Wlassow what he expected from such a late commitment of the division. Wlassow immediately saw what the German Commander in Chief wanted to know and made a truly diplomatic answer. He immediately complained of the great difficulties that had repeatedly been thrown in his path during the activation of his Russian volunteer units. His plan was to have formed an army of at least six to eight, indeed, ten divisions. His personal recruitment and propaganda among the Russian prisoners of war, especially among the Ukrainians, but also among the Caucasians

Andrej Wlassow, former Soviet general officer, captured by the Germans on
the Eastern Front and later commander of the ROA (*Russkaja Oswoboditelnaja
Armija*), or so-called *Wlassow Armee*, some of whose troops served in the
Heeresgruppe 'Weichsel' sector. (Bundesarchiv 146-1984-101-29)

and Cossacks, would have been highly successful. Hundreds of thousands would have volunteered for armed service against Russia. However, the German command had repeatedly delayed and delayed again, so that today he only had one division ready for action and a second still in the process of activation.

Obviously it was now late indeed, and the overall situation had developed unfavorably. He, too, was aware that Germany's current deplorable military situation was hardly encouraging for his volunteers. Despite all of this, he believed that he could commit the division that was ready at any time. Its state of training, which he, himself, had inspected, was good and the fighting spirit of the people the same. He had nothing but good to say about the Russian division commander, too.

He proposed that the first employment of the division be offensive. One could best test the command and troops in an attack. He considered it entirely practical to commit the division in special offensive missions in a perpetually unstable section of the front. The danger of enemy counter-propaganda, with which one now had to constantly reckon, would thus be most easily countered. Particularly the latter seemed clear and sensible to us. It did, however, contain a hidden reservation, that Wlassow, too, had some doubts as to the reliability of the division. Then Wlassow further proposed that, for its first mission, the division be given a task that it would have to carry out without help from German troops – aside from some supporting artillery. By so doing he wanted to strengthen the troops' self-confidence.

This request, or, better said, proposal, was not exactly simple to fulfil, if one wanted to avoid a potentially serious reverse. *General* Busse, however, had already anticipated such a situation. Southwest of Frankfurt there was a relatively unimportant enemy bridgehead. The enemy artillery there was weak, which provided a perfect task for a reinforced infantry regiment to attack. If the Wlassow Division attacked there, they should have an easy task. If, however, the attack was to fail, not much harm would be done. There, too, the possibility of line-crossers was minimal and withdrawal of the division after the attack would offer no complications. The *Heeresgruppe* selected this proposal from a series of alternatives. *General* Wlassow, too, considered it particularly suitable.

Accordingly, he departed from us, quite pleased, to go directly to the division. He promised to be present for the attack. We remained, however, not entirely comfortable with the thought of the impending commitment of the Russians. In my innermost thoughts I had always hoped that nothing would come of the whole matter. Now we, meaning the 9th *Armee*, would have to make the experiment.

In conclusion it is enough to state that the *Wlassow Division*, as expected, launched the attack indecisively, supported by a more-than-adequate level of German supporting artillery. Despite modest enemy resistance, the attack stalled after a few hundred meters and could not again be brought in motion. That same day Russian propaganda loud-speakers started up from the other bank of the Oder. The Commander in Chief of the 9th *Armee*, who had observed the attack, reported to *Generaloberst* Heinrici that he considered any further employment of the division would constitute a serious danger. He called for the immediate withdrawal of these troops from his *Armee* sector. All-in-all one got the impression that the Wlassow soldiers did not desire to fight any more and probably wanted a favorable opportunity to go over to their brothers on the other side. Naturally, they could most easily find such an opportunity while committed at the front.

However, even in a rear area they would always remain a dangerous factor. There was no telling whether they might suddenly turn their weapons against the rear of the German front. Therefore a simple withdrawal of this division from the front to the rear would not suffice.

That was precisely the time when the *Heeresgruppe* urgently needed weapons of all kinds to activate formations composed of *Luftwaffe* replacements. Accordingly the proposal was made to the Commander in Chief that the most useful course would be to immediately disarm the division and make better use of its weapons. Granted, that would cause bad blood with the Russians, but that seemed to us to be the simplest and, above all, a complete solution. To facilitate this disarmament, the division would be split up into separate march serials.

After a length back-and-forth the *Heeresgruppe* finally received permission from *OKH* to disarm at least some elements of the division. Its main body was transferred to *Heeresgruppe 'Schörner'*'s sector. I do not know what then happened to it there. So it was that this episode, from which Himmler had once expected so much, ran its course with no success.

OKH's objections to disarming the Russian division bordered on the laughable. All at once it was a matter of being extremely careful. The Russians would have to be handled with great care. Disarming them would put them on their honor, and so forth. To all of that one could only say: Insight entirely too late.

Part XI

In the 9th *Armee* sector, despite all efforts, not one single enemy bridgehead had been eliminated. On the contrary, in daily attacks the Russians constantly enlarged them. The situation looked particularly threatening between Frankfurt and Küstrin. In this sector the enemy had already gained so much ground west of the Oder at Lebus and across from Reitwein that he had already positioned an impressive amount of artillery, including heavy artillery, on the west bank. Facing them XI *SS Panzerkorps* clung, one could already say with toe- and finger-nails, to the Reitwein ridge. This flat plateau still commanded the Oder. If that, however, was lost, then the Russians could do whatever they wished under its protection. They would be secure from observation. The enemy command had recognized the significance of this commanding position and constantly strengthened their efforts to tear it from the grasp of the 9th *Armee*. This bitter fighting – mostly hand-to-hand for a few feet of ground – cost both sides heavy losses. The difference was that the Russians could immediately make good their losses, while, each time, we grew weaker.

The Commander in Chief of the 9th *Armee*, *General* Busse, considered that possession of the Reitweiner ridge was so decisive to his further fighting that he scraped everything together to keep that dominating terrain.[1] It was, however, only a predictable matter of time that such makeshift measures could prevail. For this reason the 9th *Armee* requested that the designation as a fortress be lifted from Frankfurt.

In this so-called fortress the garrison consisted of infantry forces with the numerical strength of about two divisions and a mass of artillery. For the time being, these forces could not even temporarily be employed at other endangered locations. So decreed Hitler's orders regarding fortifications.

General Busse argued quite simply as follows: If the Russians broke through the weak front on both sides of Frankfurt, then defense of the Oder, including the garrisoned fortress of Frankfurt, would no longer be possible. In such a situation Frankfurt would be cut off and would certainly suffer the same fate that numerous fortresses in the *Heeresgruppe* area had already met.

If, however, a portion, roughly half, of the fortress garrison, were to be immediately committed on both sides of the city at the Oder, there would be a substantially greater chance of holding the Oder sector and that part of the fortress that was situated on the west bank. *Generaloberst* Heinrici could not ignore these simple considerations. Accordingly, the *Heeresgruppe* requested that Hitler lift the fortress designation from Frankfurt with the above justification.

Predictably, this request was refused. After thorough consideration and calculations, however, it seemed so overwhelmingly vital to the 9th *Armee*, as well as to us, that we should free-up as rapidly as possible a portion of the forces in Frankfurt that *Generaloberst*

---

1 Translator's note – Tony Le Tissier gives an excellent description of the terrain in the *Oder Bruch* on pp. 43–45 of his *Zhukov at the Oder: The Decisive Battle for Berlin* and a sketch-map on p. 50 showing the village of Reitwein and the ridge, called 'The *Reitweiner-Nase*', or Reitwein 'nose' dominating the flat river bottomland terrain all around.

Heinrici requested an immediate conference with Hitler regarding this question. This request was approved. The session with Hitler took place on 6 April 1945. *Generaloberst* Heinrici ordered me to escort him. I was to bring all of the files regarding the Frankfurt fortress. That made a bulging briefcase, along with a large number of special maps. The Commander in chief clearly was preparing a general offensive against Hitler and his advisors. He was firmly resolved to force a decision in our favor.

It goes without mention that both the Commander in Chief and myself looked toward this presentation with great anxiety. Above all else the thought possessed us of the fight for the question of Frankfurt that was so vital for our troops and ourselves, and we had no doubt that it would be a battle. The thought also occurred that, within a few hours, Hitler would be back in his 'foxhole'.

Shortly after 1400 hours we arrived in the Wilhelmstrasse. I had last seen the new *Reichskanzlei* in the year before the outbreak of the war during an invitation of the *Kriegsakademie*. As I now walked through its ruined halls, the involuntary memory of Uhland's well-known poem, *Das Sängers Fluch* [*The Minstrel's Curse*], came to mind in the sense, 'Only one tall column witnesses the vanished pride; This, too, already riven, could fall this night.'[2] Nothing remained of the elegance and the rather chilly splendor that it had at my former visit. Bombed ruins. The furrowed, grief-stricken visage of most of the great cities of Germany were mirrored here. Through the wasteland of the ruin-covered gardens of the *Reichskanzlei* we made our way to the entrance of the bunker, had our identities checked by the *SS* guards and then descended the steps into the bunker. Here we were received by two young *SS* officers in a cloakroom. They politely took our coats, then, ever-so-politely, put us through a very thorough body-search. We were allowed to keep nothing on us except one handkerchief. It was humiliating to see a German *Generaloberst* and Commander in Chief go through this procedure. Obviously, my briefcase was also searched. Once before, on 20 July, a briefcase had played a very fateful role.

It was now clear to me that any sort of assassination attempt on Hitler was out of the questions, unless someone was going to strangle him with their bare hands. We were led into a sort of broad corridor which had been turned into a kind of waiting room with very beautiful furniture, carpets and pictures from the *Reichskanzlei*. There was nobody there but us. There was still about three-quarters of an hour until the situation report.

An *SS* orderly in a spotless white jacket, a giant of a man, urged us to sit down and inquired if he could offer us any sort of refreshment. The Commander in Chief asked for a cup of coffee. In a few minutes we had our coffee and some sandwiches. After the chilly journey the little snack was quite pleasant. I straightened out my files for the presentation, which had been rather disarranged by the inspection in the cloakroom. The Commander in Chief discussed several more questions for the presentation with me. At about 1430 hours there was a commotion in the anteroom. The first to appear was *General* Burgdorf, Hitler's Chief Adjutant. He welcomed us and made a few polite remarks about hoped-for good success. After Burgdorf, in short order, came Keitel, Himmler, Dönitz and Bormann. General noisy greetings. I was truly proud of my little

---

2   Translator's note – Johann Ludwig Uhland, 1787–1862, lawyer and romantic poet. Several of his poems, such as *Der Wirtin Tochterlein*, were set to music by Schubert and others. One, *'Ich hatt' einen Kameraden'*, has long been standard at military funerals. Uhland was also an active liberal in politics.

Commander in Chief in these surroundings. Serious and grave in his accustomed erect posture, from head to foot a soldier in the midst of toadies. He found a conversation that Himmler drew him into extremely unpleasant. Heinrici hated all these men in their boisterous, phony emptiness. He found Himmler especially unpleasant. He had told me that repeatedly. Accordingly he was very pleased when *General* Krebs, the Chief of the General Staff of the *Heer*, approached him in his usual self-important manner and engaged him in conversation. Himmler then conversed a few minutes with me.

Naturally, he wanted to know a mass of details about the *Heeresgruppe*. Thus I was very happy when the Commander in Chief called me to him and requested several particulars for *General* Krebs. In the meantime Keitel and Dönitz had joined them. All three promised *Generaloberst* Heinrici that they would support his justified requests to the limit. I had withdrawn from the energetically talking group a few steps and had greeted *Oberst* von Below, Hitler's *Luftwaffe* adjutant, when suddenly Bormann stepped up to us. Von Below excused himself and Bormann asked me how things stood with the *Heeresgruppe* and what I thought of the further development of the situation which was, indeed, both for Berlin and for the overall picture, of the greatest significance.

I replied that we had extremely serious concerns and, therefore, had come here today. Clapping me on the shoulder, he expressed his opinion in a consoling tone, that it would turn out all right. Certainly we would receive assistance today from the *Führer*. They knew just how important our sector on the Oder was and several more pleasant generalities. During this the broad, stocky man looked at me with his deep-set, cunning eyes as honestly and guilelessly as if he, himself, believed steadfastly in his platitudes. A cold shudder ran up my spine as I thought about the fact that this man was said to hold all the threads in his hands.

More and more people gathered in the room, which gradually seemed to grow too small and, within which, it became like a swarm of bees. *Generaloberst* Jodl came with his deputy, *Generalleutnant* Winter. As *Generaloberst* Jodl greeted us, I was again struck by the ice-cold imperturbability of this man, as I had been on the few opportunities I had previously had to meet him. The new Chief of the General Staff of the *Luftwaffe*, *General der Flieger* Koller, made a markedly unremarkable and insignificant impression. Along with this impressive number of major figures were a multitude of aids and assistants.

Suddenly the word was, 'The *Führer* is coming!' Keitel briefly specified who would take part at the *'Lage'*, [the 'Situation Briefing']. That had to be determined, for the appointed room was very small, about five meters square. Authorized for the *'Lage'* were Himmler, Bormann, Dönitz, Keitel himself, *General* Koller, *Generaloberst* Heinrici and I. We went into the situation- room immediately adjoining the anteroom and lined up. I stood between *Generaloberst* Heinrici and *Generaloberst* Jodl. The rest of the swarm of officers and other dignitaries remained outside. One would have expected that, upon Hitler's appearance, a respectful silence would have fallen. Far from it. The talking and arguing continued at a pretty high pitch. It struck me as noteworthy, but also revealing. My probably outmoded expectation was that quiet would set in when a head of state and supreme commander appeared. Either the excitement of all these gentlemen outside was so great or their respect for Hitler so small that they hardly lowered their voices. For me it felt very much like it had in a school classroom before the start of class. Then *General* Burgdorf stepped into the situation room and said: 'Gentlemen, the *Führer* comes.'

At that moment Hitler entered through the door. Everyone raised their hand in the German salute. Outside one could still hear – somewhat muffled – the confusion of numerous voices. Hitler moved along the row of those attending, silent, somewhat bent over, his steps dragging, if not to say slinking, giving his hand to each. This hand, which still ruled the German people, was soft, slack – one hardly felt it. Hitler's face was bloated, unhealthy. His eyes stared fixedly at one without any expression. He let himself fall into the armchair before the map-table like a sack and sat there, remaining silent and deflated, arms resting on the arms of the chair.

In addition to the great map table and Hitler's armchair there was a simple wooden bench behind the table on the other side. Himmler, Dönitz and Keitel sat on the bench. All the others stood around the table. Keitel, who obviously took care of the necessary honours, reported to Hitler that the Commander in Chief of *Heeresgruppe 'Weichsel'* and his first general staff officer were there. At that point Krebs suggested that, for this reason, the situation briefing should start with *Heeresgruppe 'Weichsel'* so that *Generaloberst* Heinrici could put forward his request and be able to return promptly to his *Heeresgruppe*. Krebs further suggested that the Commander in Chief of the *Heeresgruppe*, himself, report on his situation.

Hitler, still completely apathetic, nodded his head and gestured with his hand to *Generaloberst* Heinrici, who then stepped up to the map table and began his situation briefing. During this we stood on both sides of Hitler. *Generaloberst* Heinrici initially described the current overall situation of the *Heeresgruppe*. As always, his talk was brief, clear, to the point and, one might say, dryly down-to-earth.

Within about 15 minutes he had given a clear picture. Everyone listened attentively. There was not one interruption. He then asked Hitler if he could explain his particular concerns about the 9th *Armee* and the question of the Frankfurt Fortress.

Again there was only a curt nod from Hitler, who sat there as if detached, starring at the map. It seemed almost as if Hitler had, to that point, not even listened.

In dealing with the Frankfurt situation, Heinrici became more animated. It was clear how this matter moved him and how important it was to him. During this presentation Hitler seemed to wake up and, in a soft voice that seemed to me completely unlike his usual tones, asked several technical questions about strengths, ammunition, weapons and the like.

At this point Heinrici involved me and my files in the conversation. Hitler examined the material laid before him and requested further explanations here and there, particularly over the concentration of the fortress artillery. In general, he seemed entirely agreeable.

He turned to the Chief of the General Staff of the Army and said to him: 'Krebs, the opinion of the *Herr Generaloberst* in the matter of the Frankfurt Fortress seems quite correct. Prepare the appropriate orders for the *Heeresgruppe* and give them to me today.' Heinrici looked at me over Hitler's head and his look told me what a load had fallen from his heart.

At that moment we heard a commotion outside, the door flew open and *Herr Reichsmarschall* Göring burst in. He loudly greeted Hitler and the others present, rather briefly excused himself to Hitler, who had given him his hand, for his late appearance, and then had Krebs briefly fill him in. Then, as was his wont, he placed both hands on the map-table and, probably with all good intentions of helping us, started to tell of a visit that he had just made to the 9th *Fallschirmjägerdivision* at the Oder Front.

In this instant something occurred that was, at least to *Generaloberst* Heinrici and myself, totally unexpected. Hitler abruptly straightened up and suddenly erupted like a volcano. Screaming loudly he suddenly began to complain about his generals and advisors who did not want to understand him. Here, too, in the question of fortresses he only ran into incomprehension. However, history had lessons to teach, and now followed numerous, rapid-fire and often vague, historical examples, such as, for example, Kolberg, Prague and many others. In this war, too, he continued, the fortresses had accomplished their missions. That could be said of Breslau, Posen and Schneidemühl. How many enemy forces had they tied down and how much trouble had they caused the Russians? He well knew why he had the fortresses fight to the last man. Therefore Frankfurt must remain a fortress.

Just as quickly as it had begun this outbreak came to an end, only Hitler could no longer sit still. His entire body seemed to tremble. The hands, in which he held several drawing pencils struck out and down wildly, rattling the pencils on the wood of the armrests. The entire man gave the impression of one who is seriously insane. To me it all seemed totally unreal, and it seemed incomprehensible that this ruin of a man should now decide the fate of an entire people.

Generaloberst Heinrici, however, did not yet give up his fight for lost. With a voice that was just as calm and firm as the other's had been loud and shaking, he again emphasized the decisive importance of freeing up a portion of the forces held fast in Frankfurt for the further fighting of the *Heeresgruppe*. Thereupon Himmler, Göring and Dönitz joined in and attempted rather ineptly to second *Generaloberst* Heinrici.

Hitler only wearily waved his hand and began to ask questions about the fortress that had actually been exhaustively answered during the preceding presentation. Suddenly he became especially interested in the character of the fortress commandant.

Generaloberst Heinrici replied that the Commandant, *Oberst* Bieler, was a particularly reliable officer who had been repeatedly proven in the field. He had reported voluntarily from a Frankfurt hospital before he had even completely healed to the first Commandant at the start of the construction of the fortress. In the course of time he became the driving force in the fortress. For this reason he was appointed successor when the first Commandant fell ill. He, as the Commander in Chief of the *Heeresgruppe,* and the Commander in Chief of the 9th *Armee*, too, were convinced that the fortress of Frankfurt was in the right hands with this man.

In response Hitler only asked, "Is he a Gneisenau?"[3]

---

3   Translator's note – August *Graf* Neidhart von Gneisenau, (1760–1831) was one of Prussia's most distinguished soldiers. Of the many valorous episodes in his life, Hitler here was referring to the time, in 1807, during the Napoleonic wars, when, early in 1807, as fortress commander in Kolberg, the then-*Major* von Gneisenau led the small and poorly protected city and its garrison in successfully holding out against superior French forces until the Peace of Tilsit, for which he was awarded the *Pour le Mérite* and promoted to *Oberstleutnant*. This historical reference had particular significance in that the Nazi propaganda organization had just produced a movie spectacular about that siege of Kolberg, hoping to inspire fortress-garrisons in general, and that of Kolberg in particular, to hold out to the last man 'for the Fatherland' and in hopes of a repeat of the historical successful outcome of the siege of Kolburg in 1807.

Even this astounding question did not shake *Generaloberst* Heinrici's composure. Cool and calm was his answer: *Oberst* Bieler would only prove whether he was a Gneisenau in the actual battle for Frankfurt. As his Commander in Chief, however, he Heinrici vouched for him.

Hitler then required that the Commandant of the Frankfurt Fortress report to him personally on the following day. He would form his own personal impression of him and, at that time, decide the question of whether Frankfurt should remain a fortress. With that the first, and probably the last, round of our fight was lost. Neither *Generaloberst* Jodl nor *General* Krebs had made any attempt to support my Commander in Chief. They stood aside and observed the mood of their lord and master. In contrast, *General* Krebs now vigorously joined in to assure the ordered visit of *Oberst* Bieler.

Hitler then spoke of the bombing of the Russian bridges over the Oder. *Generaloberst* Heinrici dryly observed that they were, indeed, bombed daily but with little success. That led to a technical discussion of some kind of bomb between Hitler and the Chief of the General Staff of the *Luftwaffe,* Koller. This poor man was unable to give a suitable answer, was shortly out of his depth and hastily vanished with his tail between his legs to fetch some documents, a shameful but revealing sidelight.

Göring now joined in and soon there was a palaver going on about this relatively trivial thing. *Generaloberst* Heinrici then took his leave, Hitler shook our hands and we left the room in which Germany's destiny would be guided and decided. In the antechamber we were informed that an air-raid alarm had been sounded. Nobody would be allowed to leave the bunker until the all-clear was sounded. We sat down at a small table and waited, without speaking a word. We were too preoccupied with thoughts of what had just taken place.

After some time Kaltenbrunner appeared, with Speer. They greeted us and sat down with us. The usually so well-controlled countenance of my Commander in Chief clearly expressed his unconcealed distaste with the new company. Eventually the all-clear sounded and we could go out into the fresh air, which I had hardly ever perceived as such a great blessing.

When we were in the car, my Commander in Chief, who had not yet spoken a word, turned to me, gazed deeply and seriously at me with his great blue eyes and only said, "It has come to this. It is all futile now". I did not answer. Probably no answer was expected. Only later in our return journey did the Commander in Chief speak with me about the visit of the Commandant of Frankfurt to Hitler. He did not expect anything to come of it but, in any case, he wanted to speak beforehand with *Oberst* Bieler.

General Kinzel anxiously awaited our return. In a long, serious discussion with the Chief of the General Staff and myself the Commander in Chief said, regarding our recent experience, that we could no longer expect any rational actions from Hitler or his military advisers. He then telephoned the Commander in Chief of the 9th *Armee*, briefly filled him in on the failure and ordered that *Oberst* Bieler immediately proceed via the *Heeresgruppe* to Berlin.

General Busse objected with good reason that one could not rouse the Fortress Commandant who was constantly on his feet all day, in the night and hasten him off to us and then to Hitler. He, too, would have to talk briefly with *Oberst* Bieler and a little collection and preparation was required to prepare this officer, who was at just this time especially overloaded, for such an important occasion. Thereupon *General* Kinzel telephoned the Chief of the General Staff of the *Heer* and requested, for the reasons stated above, that the visit of the Commandant of Frankfurt be postponed by one day.

General Krebs seemed to understand the reasons and promised to effect the change. However, half an hour later *General* Burgdorf called back and informed us that Hitler required that the Commandant come to the next day's situation briefing. Therefore *Oberst* Bieler had to leave Frankfurt that evening and got to us late at night.

He truly appeared to be totally exhausted and overworked. The Commander in Chief discussed again with him the situation of Frankfurt in detail and the *Heeresgruppe's* requests. The following morning *Oberst* Bieler, accompanied with our best wishes, drove to Berlin. He was to report directly to the Commander in Chief on his way back.

Late that afternoon *General* Burgdorf telephoned that *Oberst* Bieler had not made much of an impression on Hitler. Certainly he was no Gneisenau. Hitler had ordered his immediate relief. The new Commandant would be appointed by the Personnel Bureau [*Personalamt*]. *General* Burgdorf could not or would not give the Commander in Chief any details regarding this sudden action.

Generaloberst Heinrici was furious to the extreme. He wished only to wait for Bieler's report before engaging in countermeasures. *Oberst* Bieler reported on his visit as follows:

After arriving in the bunker at the *Reichskanzlei* he had to wait in the anteroom about two hours. Due to the heat there and his exhaustion he probably fell asleep in the armchair. He was then suddenly awakened by *General* Burgdorf and taken to Hitler. Hitler gave him his hand, exchanged a few trivial words and then sent him off. Nothing was discussed about Fortress Frankfurt. He knew nothing about his relief until he heard it from us.

To fully understand this, perhaps trivial appearing, but typical matter, it must be pointed out that *Oberst* Bieler wore spectacles and did not exactly give the external impression of a Nordic warrior.

In Bieler's presence the Commander in Chief telephoned first *General* Burgdorf and then *General* Krebs. He expressed to both in no-uncertain terms his fury over the entire incredible affair. He demanded from each of them the immediate suspension of the relief of *Oberst* Bieler. Otherwise, he, as Commander in Chief of the *Heeresgruppe*, would draw his own conclusions. He refused to accept any other Commandant for Frankfurt on technical grounds. He expected an appropriate decision that very day.

After these conversations he dictated a teletype message in which he requested the immediate awarding of the *Ritterkreuz* to *Oberst* Bieler. *Oberst* Bieler had, in fact, been put in for this decoration months earlier as a result of his success as commander of an infantry regiment.

Some time later *General* Burgdorf called the Chief of the General Staff and demanded that he talk the Commander in Chief into changing his mind. Bieler must be relieved. Hitler required it. *General* Kinzel refused to take any part in the matter. As noon drew near that day two teletypes arrived at the *Heeresgruppe* from the *Führerhauptquartier*. In the first *Oberst* Bieler was confirmed in his position as Commandant of Frankfurt. In the second he was awarded the long-overdue *Ritterkreuz*.

Thus *Generaloberst* Heinrici had, at least in the question of the Commandant of Fortress Frankfurt, won a total victory. However, in the decisive question whether Frankfurt was to remain a fortress or not, it was impossible to achieve a change. Frankfurt remained a fortress. Its controversial Commandant fell, so far as I remember, in the defense of Frankfurt, thereby proving that he understood how to fight like a Gneisenau

This entire episode of Frankfurt has been so extensively described because it reveals how Hitler and his advisors generally judged men whom they did not even know. The initial external appearance was all that mattered. There was no talk of anything technical. How many valuable assets had Hitler damned for their external appearances and put on the shelf?

Part XII

R oughly at the end of March and the beginning of April the *Heeresgruppe* found itself in the situation of a rabbit that stares as if frozen in place at a snake that is about to eat it. It cannot move a limb, only wait for the moment when the snake will strike with lightning speed. At the start of April the Russian command completed its preparations for the Berlin offensive. Each day we expected the attack to begin. It was vital, even in our hopeless situation, to correctly recognize the start date, for the few measures that were possible in our weakness, required a certain time. Above all, that was required for a certain amount of regrouping.

Generaloberst Heinrici refused to accept that the *Heeresgruppe* was no longer able, with its own forces, to take any significant action. At least a hundred times he had weighed all the possibilities with the Chief of the General Staff and myself for strengthening the front of the 9th *Armee* and for providing it with at least a few local reserves, without further weakening the already-too-weak 3rd *Panzerarmee*.

Even if one were to accept every risk between the Hohenzollern Canal and Stettin, a security garrison would still have to remain there to conduct some sort of watch over the river. In this sector it was requisite to at least discover when and where the Russians crossed the river, the more so since, following the loss of the Stettin bridgehead, there were signs of an impending Russian attack there, too. From the viewpoint of the Russian command it was obvious that they should attack on the widest possible front. That would make it impossible for the *Heeresgruppe*, for their part, to form any kind of a defensive *Schwerpunkt*. The Russians could, truly, play with us like a cat with a mouse.

Much was also said about this apparently insoluble problem once again when Göring was with us. He recognized this difficulty and promised to do the utmost to provide us with reinforcements. As a result of his efforts in conjunction with Dönitz at the start of April the *Heeresgruppe* received advance notice of about 30,000 replacements from the personnel of the *Luftwaffe* and navy. We immediately inquired when we could count on the arrival of these replacements and what we could expect so far as level of training, average age and, above all, armament and equipment.

OKH remained stubbornly silent about this question. Finally, however, we received transport lists and, since we still knew nothing about the condition of these replacements, we were ordered to initially assemble them in the rear areas of the two armies in empty barracks and *RAD* [*Reichsarbeitsdienst, Reichs* labor service] camps and look them over.

When the first transports arrived, the armies reported that the replacements consisted of the best of human material, meaning quite young age classes, but that they were neither trained nor, in any way, armed. Indeed, some of them were not even properly clothed for active duty.

Immediately the *Armeen* and *Heeresgruppe* instituted all conceivable measures to meet the most serious deficiencies. It soon proved, however, that there was no way of arming these men. There was no longer any German armaments industry, nor were there any sort of stocks on hand. At that time we gathered up every weapon. We were barely able to come up with a thousand rifles. That would hardly suffice for 30,000 men. Therefore the Commander in Chief ordered that the replacements remain in the barracks and camps and that training proceed as best it could without weapons.

Hitler, who apparently believed that, with these 30,000 men, the *Heeresgruppe* had now been saved, demanded an exact report as to how and where these soldiers were to be committed. I immediately called the *OKH* Operations Section and reported that the replacements could not be committed in action since we had no weapons for them. At the same time I again requested at least the necessary small-arms.

OKH, of course, also had no weapons and the Chief of the Operations Section understood that one could not commit unarmed soldiers. Later that very day a sharply-worded teletype arrived from the Chief of the General Staff of the *Heer* again demanding immediate commitment and even detailed information on the organization of the replacements. *Generaloberst* Heinrici looked blankly at the Chief and myself and said, 'Kinzel, tell this Krebs yet again that we need weapons.' *General* Kinzel spoke with Krebs and then we had to experience the fact that, after a bit of back-and-forth, *General* Krebs suddenly said, 'The *Führer* demands that these men be committed. Therefore it must be done. We expect an appropriate report from the *Heeresgruppe*.'

It was, indeed, possible, if incomprehensible, that Hitler, in the condition he was at that time, wanted unarmed men to be sent into action. What was, however, beyond understanding was that the Chief of the General Staff of the *Heer*, who was neither insane nor drunk, also demanded that. Several more extremely heated discussions took place with *OKH*, in which I was no longer in a state where I could maintain the requisite politeness. The end result was a written order from Hitler to immediately commit the replacements in the second position and report on their organization.

That meant, to put it plainly, that untrained, unarmed men with no field experience were to sit in foxholes four to five kilometers behind the front line and wait for what was to come. They could not even dig in sensibly, since there were no digging tools. *OKH* had, in addition, as Columbus's egg, ordered that these replacements were each to be armed with two *Panzerfäuste*. That was how clever we had become. Yet one could not help asking, what does a man do in an open field when, with more or less success, he has fired these two *Panzerfäuste* at enemy armour and infantry? He then takes the discharged barrel of the *Panzerfaust* like a cudgel and charges the enemy, who is armed to the teeth. One need hardly inquire about the outcome. This was simply an order for systematic mass murder, nothing less.

The *Heeresgruppe* did not carry out this order. A skeleton-garrison, selected from these replacements, was committed in the second position and, indeed, as many soldiers as could be more-or-less armed and provided with entrenching tools, so that appearances could be maintained in the event of some sort of inspection by *OKH*.

The *Heeresgrupppe* had, in addition, asked Göring, himself, to convince Hitler of the impossibility of this order. Göring did, himself, see the grotesqueness of the situation, promised everything and accomplished nothing. In this order, too, which undoubtedly came from Hitler, one can again see the traitorous and senseless madness of Hitler, who wanted to drag down as many as possible of his people with him in his downfall.

The fact that the *Reichs* capital, Berlin, was in its rear area became an ever-increasing concern for the *Heeresgruppe*. Berlin was subject in every respect, even regarding its possible defense, to special directives issued by Hitler. Even in the early days when I was still under Himmler as Commander in Chief, it was clear to me that, one day, despite all the special directives, responsibility for this great city would fall on the *Heeresgruppe*. Accordingly, at that time it already seemed vital to, at least, be briefed about the military preparations and, if possible, have some influence on them.

Himmler and the then-Chief of Staff, Lammerding, were in agreement that we should orientate ourselves in a quite general sort of way on the military preparations in Berlin. By chance and good luck I happened to personally know *Generalleutnant* Reimann, who was, at that time, Commandant of Berlin, as well as his Chief of General Staff, *Oberst i.G.* Refior. In particular, the latter was in my age-class. So I telephoned *Generalleutnant* Reimann and *Oberst* Refior at the beginning of March and it was arranged that, initially, *Oberst* Refior would bring his files to the *Heeresgruppe* to give us a picture of the conditions in Berlin.

Refior arrived with a pile of papers, his files. Right from the start, I held no great expectations. The bare and unvarnished facts, however, that he laid before me were simply appalling. On the map, Berlin was divided into several defensive belts or zones, and these zones, in turn, divided into a number of sectors.

As I remember, the outermost zone ran roughly along the so-called '*Berliner-Ringes*' of the *Reichsautobahn*. That had an extent of about 150 kilometers. It was clear that there was nothing to be done with this outer zone. It would have required the forces of an *Armee* of about ten divisions for its defense.

The next zone followed the so-called 'outer edge of the city'. This, too, extended about 90 kilometers. Then came two more belts, the one roughly following the city commuter-train ring, about 40 kilometers long, and a narrower inner one around the government quarter.

As far as construction of defensive positions for these four zones, all the preparations that had been made by the *Reichsverteidigungskommissar* [Reichs- Defense-Commissar] were totally inadequate and amateurish. As everywhere, the first priority had been given to anti-tank obstacles, whose value, or lack thereof, has already been discussed. Only a few field positions existed. At that time, however, several had been constructed. Now, however, the best positions are of no avail unless they can be adequately garrisoned, whereby one comes to the question of forces.

In that respect things looked even worse. At the time of this first briefing the troops available to the Commandant of the 'Greater-Berlin Fortress System', as it existed on paper, comprised, so far as regular troops, two guard battalions[1] and a few pioneer companies. Then there were about 25–30 *Volkssturm* battalions as infantry. Their armament was deplorable, adequate in neither rifles, machine guns nor mortars. There were also a few so-called fortress-anti-tank units, and, aside from the regular Berlin *Flak* defenses, a miserable artillery. The latter appeared to have been collected from the inventories of venerable arsenals.

The *Volkssturm* was poorly trained and over-age. Above all, the command situation gave greatest cause for concern, since suitable officers were unavailable. Thus the entire defense preparations of the *Reichs* capital city seemed more like a Mardi-Gras jest. The desperation of the Commandant and his Chief of staff regarding this condition were entirely understandable.

---

1   Translator's note – *Wach-bataillone* were guard, or watch, battalions for guard service in rear or interior zones, in no way to be confused with 'The Guards' or the élite Soviet Guards units.

When I asked what *OKH* had to say about it *Oberst* Refior replied, 'Nothing at all.' The *Führer* had exclusive control, and he had only said to *Generalleutnant* Reimann that, if it ever got to that point, adequate forces would be available from the troops fighting around Berlin. At that time there had also been talk of several *Panzer* divisions. Neither of us said more about that prospect, but merely looked at each other.

After that first discussion it was said that the *Heeresgruppe* would be continually kept up to date on the current state of things with respect to the defense of Berlin. That took place, but it only revealed that practically nothing positive was being done. The so-called garrison of 'Fortress Berlin' consisted, as before, of 90% *Volkssturm*. After several thorough discussions with the Commander in Chief and the Chief of the General Staff regarding the possible further development of the situation in the case of a Russian breakthrough, I maintained from the start that the *Heeresgruppe* had to concentrate its entire forces in the area north of Berlin to build a defensive flank facing south between the Oder and Elbe rivers in the general line Hohenzollern Canal – Neustettin[2] – Havelberg, provided that, in the meantime, the Anglo-Americans had not crossed the Elbe and attacked us from the rear.

With this in mind it was obviously vital to prevent strong forces of the *Heeresgruppe*, especially the 9th *Armee*, from being forced aside to Berlin or to our neighbour adjoining on the right, *Heeresgruppe 'Schörner'* in Silesia. I considered that the worst possible situation would be for the 9th *Armee* to fall back on the *Reichs* capital, for that would give Hitler the opportunity to complete his fortress orgy, which he had opened with Stalingrad, by closing it with Berlin.

That must be prevented at all costs. A battle for Berlin had no military purpose. It could not bring about any change in the desperate overall situation, but would cause unforeseeable misery for a city of over a million and its population, which had already suffered quite enough from the terror bombing. The lunatic in the bunker could no longer be allowed responsibility for the suffering of innocent women and children, especially by those who could provide him with the final cards for such a frivolous game. That was, in the first line, *Heeresgruppe 'Weichsel'*. Such thoughts and considerations would normally be high treason. But what else had the direction of the war in the last year by Hitler been with regard to the German people?

Generaloberst Heinrici was too confirmed a Prussian officer to have been able to come lightly and easily to such considerations. Both *General* Kinzel and I had to watch the serious inner battle of our Commander in Chief. We did everything possible, so far as it lay within our feeble powers, to help him overcome the heavy burden of doubt. He made no use of our help, but overcame it on his own. At the end of March he had the Commandant of Berlin and his Chief of Staff come to another discussion with us. In addition to the Chief of the *Heeresgruppe* General Staff and myself, *Reichsminister* Speer also took part. *Generaloberst* Heinrici bluntly told the Commandant of Berlin that he could not count on support from *Heeresgruppe 'Weichsel'*, since that would inevitably be used for other necessary objectives. Even if, in the case of a Russian breakthrough to Berlin, *OKH* ordered elements of the *Heeresgruppe* to be turned aside to Berlin, he would not be able to count on that order being fulfilled, since experience had shown that

2   Translator's note – Possibly the author is referring to Neustadt.

breakthrough battles created massive disorder and planned dispositions had to be altered under the pressure of circumstance.

Generalleutnant Reimann answered that, in that case, he no longer knew how he should defend Berlin. It would then come to the demolition measures ordered by Hitler in case of an attack on the city. As would, actually, be the case everywhere, all of the bridges over the Spree, Havel and also other railroad, city commuter and elevated railway bridges were to be demolished. There were special instructions regarding the demolition of the underground railway system.

Generalleutnant Reimann informed us that the requisite preparations had already been made. The big problem would be, in a serious situation, to issue the demolition order in time but not unnecessarily, since his only communications network was the postal telephone system and far too few *Ordonnanzoffiziere* were available to him. This was the question that had, for a long time, been his most serious concern. *Generaloberst* Heinrici said to him in that regard that he considered all demolitions in Berlin useless for any military purpose, but entirely too deadly for the life of the giant city. If *Heeresgruppe* 'Weichsel' was placed in command over Berlin, he would forbid all demolition measures.

Thereupon *Generalleutnant* Reimann looked at the Commander in Chief with some confusion and only answered that these demolitions had been ordered by the *Führer*. At this point Minister Speer joined in the conversation and eloquently described to the *General* what effect just the destruction of the bridges of the outer districts would have on Berlin. The entire electric and water supply would fail, since they essentially came into the city from outside along these bridges. Furthermore, the entire transportation network would collapse. With that the supply of this giant city, even after it was occupied by the enemy, would be crippled for months, perhaps for years. As the result of this failure immeasurable plague, hunger and thirst could be expected for a population of a million innocent, helpless people. It was the duty of the Commandant of Berlin and underlay his joint responsibility to prevent such a catastrophe, knowing that to do so would run counter to Hitler's orders.

A serious conflict took place in *Generalleutnant* Reimann. Finally he answered in a hoarse voice that, hitherto, he had played his part in the war as an upright and honorable German officer. His son had fallen in the face of the enemy. He had lost his homeland and his home. He would, at least, keep his honor. He particularly pointed out the fate of the pioneer officer who had failed to demolish the Rhine bridge at Remagen in time. That officer had been executed like a dishonourable criminal, smearing his name for all time.

Both *Generaloberst* Heinrici and Speer, too, urgently tried again to dispel these personal reservations of the Commandant. *Generalleutnant* Reimann could not yet find the determination to refuse to obey Hitler's demolition orders. A merciful fate would later spare him from it. By the time the attack started he was the Commandant of Potsdam and was no longer responsible for Berlin.

Part XIII

On about 12 April 1945 the 9th *Armee* reported that the Russian offensive against its front could be expected any day. In particular, movements of armour had been observed in the enemy bridgeheads on both sides of Küstrin during the last few days. Registration of enemy artillery was another sign that the start of the attack was immediately imminent. Another sign was the increase in activity by the Russian air force against the rear of the frontal area.

After his short visit to the Oder Front Hitler personally promised the Commander in Chief of the 9th *Armee* help for the expected defensive battle. It now arrived in the form of LVI *Panzerkorps*. On about 10 April this *Korps* was withdrawn from *Heeresgruppe* 'Schörner's' area in Silesia and sent to *Heeresgruppe* 'Weichsel' for employment in the area of the 9th *Armee*. The *Korps* consisted of the divisions already known from Stargard, *Panzerdivisionen* 'Frundsberg' [9th *SS Panzerdivision* 'Frundsberg'], 'Führer-Grenadier-Division' and the 18th *Panzerdivision*. In addition *Panzerdivision* 'Kurmark' came from the 9th *Armee*. The divisions were sent by rail to the Fürstenwalde – Müncheberg area.

The *General des Transportwesens* of the *Heeresgruppe* [officer in charge of transport movements] *Oberst i.G.* Hamberger, provided us with a very interesting and graphic picture of the transport movements of the *Panzer* divisions in the *Heeresgruppe* 'Weichsel' territory. His description showed that several divisions had wandered around on the railroad system for up to 21 days to provide a total of four to five actual days in action with us and *Heeresgruppe* 'Schörner'. That was for journeys, the longest of which was about 250 kilometers. That illustrates, on the one hand, the difficulties of our railroad situation and, on the other, the hopeless fuel situation at that time.

In normal times one would never have loaded the wheeled elements of *Panzer* divisions on the railroad for such urgent movements over such relatively short distances – often only 40 to 50 kilometers. Now precious time was sacrificed to spare even more precious fuel. The four *Panzer* divisions in question had all been badly battered in the previous fighting and amounted, all together, to about one-and-one-half full *Panzer*-divisions. They were to constitute the mobile reserve of the 9th *Armee* that had been demanded from time immemorial behind its overextended front.

Originally the *Armee* had requested three mobile reserve groups, a southern group in the area west of Frankfurt, a central[group in the Seelow – Werbig area and a northern group in the sector northwest of Küstrin, roughly in the Wriezen area. Depending on the situation, these groups could then be concentrated. Now, however, the forces were insufficient for such grouping if one was to avoid fragmentation of forces. Therefore the *Heeresgruppe* and *Armee* had to decide, with heavy hearts, to form only one group approximately behind the center. That made timely employment behind the south or north wing questionable.

The command of the *Heeresgruppe*, especially the Commander in Chief, was in constant self-torment over the problem of additional infantry reinforcement of the 9th *Armee* front. This problem, however, was on a par with squaring the circle. Where there is nothing, the *Kaiser* has lost his power [an old saying]. So it was for us here. Nevertheless, at the daily situation briefings every possibility was weighed anew, how to somehow yet scrape up a battalion to give to the 9th *Armee* for use at the front.

When fighting started in the Reitwein bridgehead and at Frankfurt the Commander in Chief spoke to me, cross, and in utter desperation, 'What can you think of, *Ia*? You *must* think of some way that we can support the 9th *Armee*. By this evening something will occur to you and you will give me your proposal.' *General* Kinzel consoled me and said that he, too, could think of nothing. Plain and simply, we had nothing more to commit, and any further withdrawal of even so much as one or two battalions from the front of the 3rd *Panzerarmee* could no longer be countenanced. It would leave a gap in the front.

From the very beginning, the Russians conducted the offensive that opened against Berlin on 15 April with extreme commitment of men and matériel. The artillery fire opened up with a strength and weight such as we had only hitherto experienced in the great battles of extermination in the East. With hardly a pause the enemy pounded with all calibers not only the front line, but also the rear of the frontal area. This artillery fire was overlaid with heavy forces from the continually attacking Russian air force. This overwhelming fire alone smashed the front line in short order. Deep enemy penetrations were reported almost everywhere.

Immediately the *Heeresgruppe* occupied the forward command post that had been previously prepared for this attack in Dammühle, in the area west of Strausberg. The Commander in Chief, with a small command echelon consisting of the *Ia* and *Ic*, along with several *Ordonnanzoffiziere*, clerks and draftsmen, commanded from there. The Chief of the General Staff with the main body of the staff remained at the Hassleben command post at Prenzlau. Already on the second day it became clear that this advanced command post was impractical. As was always the case at this sort of advanced command post for higher commands many of the records necessary for command were not there. The Chief of the General Staff was nearly eliminated from the effective command structure. The only actual advantage was that the Commander in Chief could get to the front more rapidly. In the event this single advantage failed to outweigh the many disadvantages of a divided command instrument. Accordingly, on the second day the *Ia* had to go back to Hassleben, and, one day later, the Commander in Chief also realized that only from there could he effectively command.

Part XIV

It is now necessary to turn to Hitler's plans that he had formed for the case of an attack on the capital city of the *Reich* and the splitting of the remainder of Germany into two parts. In March Hitler had already considered this possibility. Obviously it could not deter him from fighting on to final victory. However, a new headquarters for Hitler and the *Reichs* government would have to be found. He therefore resolved that, in the event of the '*Reich*' being split, he and the government, *OKW* [*Oberkommando der Wehrmacht*, Armed Forces High Command] and *OKH* [*Oberkommando des Heeres*, Army High Command] would go to southern Germany, thereby placing himself in the protecting arms of his last-named *Feldmarschall*, Schörner. He intended that Dönitz serve as Regent and military Commander in Chief of the northern part.

Preparations therefore were immediately set in motion. Accordingly, most of the government offices and portions of the military command apparatus were transferred to southern Germany, essentially to Bavaria in the Garmisch area. One of the first to go was *Reichsmarschall* Hermann Göring, who went to southern Germany, where he considered himself to be Hitler's deputy until the *Führer* himself arrived. Hitler, himself, wanted to remain in Berlin as long as possible

Großadmiral Dönitz began with the activation of a new command staff. As his Chief of the General Staff, he chose *General der Infanterie* Kinzel (who was, in the meantime, promoted to that rank). In brief, *Heeresgruppe 'Weichsel'* thus received its third Chief of General Staff in barely three months. *Generaloberst* Heinrici and I were hardly pleased to lose such a competent Chief of the General Staff. Above all, Hitler's entire plan for the split command seemed to be only a final farce, to save face.

Neither was *General* Kinzel very happy over the prospect of his new position. Nevertheless, all preparations were attended to. Since Kinzel had to go to Dönitz frequently, he was now only half present at the *Heeresgruppe*. Accordingly, again a part of the work of the Chief of the General Staff fell upon the *Ia*. In the meantime in the *Führer* bunker Hitler's paladins pressed for the move to southern Germany. Above all, Bormann and *General* Krebs daily attempted to persuade Hitler to leave Berlin.

Suddenly, however, Hitler came to a new resolution. He wanted to remain in Berlin to wait there for the inevitable end. There could no longer be anything more than awaiting the end. Granted, it was still possible to order a thousand things, but, each day, these orders became ever more senseless. So it came that Hitler was cut off in Berlin by his own choice and permitted nobody to deter him from his final resolution to give everything up for lost. He permitted nearly all his political and military advisors to leave him. So far as is known, the only important people to remain with him in the bunker were Goebbels and his family, Bormann, *Generale* Krebs and Burgdorf and several adjutants. In addition there was his bodyguard of the *Waffen-SS*. With Hitler's decision to remain in Berlin, the already-prepared organization of the two remaining sections of Germany, north and south, became moot. Hitler continued to rule and order from the bunker without consideration for the ever-tighter encirclement by the Russians.

In this situation his two most faithful followers believed that they had to act on their own. *Reichsmarschall* Göring considered that the legally established succession was already in effect, and Heinrich Himmler believed he had to make a last attempt at peace negotiations through Sweden. Both would draw upon themselves the anathema of the dying dictator. In one of the usual unbridled hate-filled orders they were stripped of all offices and honors and were, doubtless, to be executed. However, the man in the bunker no longer had the power to accomplish that.

In the time remaining before his final end, aside from orders within the *Reichs* capital, itself, Hitler only issued orders to two men: *Feldmarschall* Schörner in the south and *Großadmiral* Dönitz in the north.

In Berlin, in the meantime, the third Commandant had been named. He was an *Oberst* whose name I have forgotten. Within three days he had been promoted to *Generalmajor* and *Generalleutnant* and provided with all conceivable powers by Hitler. These legal and military jurisdictional powers, however, were the only power that was available to him. It was useless against the Russian armour.

But now back to the situation of *Heeresgruppe 'Weichsel'*. Following the breakthrough in 9th *Armee's* sector toward Berlin the most important mission of the *Heeresgruppe* had to be saving this *Armee* from imminent encirclement. The grounds for this have already been explained. The Russians had, in the meantime, achieved what one could well call another breakthrough from the Cottbus area aimed at Berlin in the sector of the adjoining *Heeresgruppe 'Schörner'*.

This enemy thrust between the Spree and Elbe Rivers seemed aimed less at the southern part of Berlin and far more at Potsdam, thereby swinging around west of Berlin. At the same time, however, this Russian advance seriously endangered the deep southern flank and rear of the 9th *Armee*, which was still holding firm with elements at the Oder and south of Frankfurt. There was no more time to lose if one was to avoid standing by idly while an army was cut off without rhyme or reason.

An appropriate evaluation of the situation was given to *OKH* by the Commander in Chief of *Heeresgruppe 'Weichsel'*. At that point *OKH* was located with *OKW* in Rheinsberg. Rheinsberg had been the alternate command post for *Heeresgruppe 'Weichsel'* and had been prepared by the *Heeresgruppe*. Now we had to make new and inadequate preparations for a new alternate command post.

From the outset the *Heeresgruppe* wanted it to be in the Mecklenburg area, near Güstrow – Schwerin. *General* Krebs rejected the *Heeresgruppe* evaluation. He said that the *Führer* had ordered the 9th *Armee* to hold at the Oder. The fate of Berlin depended on this *Armee*. Supposedly, so long as the 9th *Armee* remained in the area south of Frankfurt, the Russians would be unable to carry out an orderly attack on Berlin. Once again, the 9th *Armee* 'fixed' strong Russian forces that would otherwise attack Berlin. In addition, measures were introduced to relieve this *Armee* and, thereby, Berlin. The new *Panzerarmee 'Wenck'*, at that time on its approach march in the South Harz area, would, in a few days, arrive for the decisive relief attack.

That was something entirely new, which the *Heeresgruppe* had hitherto been unable to include in its calculations. It would have been something approaching a joyful surprise in this hopeless situation if one had not suspected what was hiding behind these great plans. In accord with the development of the situation to our rear, regarding the Anglo-Americans, it seemed remarkable to the *Heeresgruppe* that suddenly, just there, a new *Armee*, and, moreover, a *Panzerarmee*, was on its approach march. The situation there appeared exceedingly obscure to us. The reports that we received from *OKH* were meager, mostly outdated and extremely imprecise. Despite daily questions regarding them we received no clear information.

The closer the enemy approached the Elbe and, therefore, our rear, the more energetically the *Heeresgruppe* pressed for clear orientation. To no avail. We got the impression that the intention was to keep the command of the *Heeresgruppe* artificially in ignorance in order to prevent them from having any concern because of the situation to their rear, as a way of strengthening their will to resist to the East. This intentional concealment– or, better put, deception – practice in the neo-German Military Command had frequently rebounded on itself in the most bitter manner. How many false decisions had been made in this war because the Supreme Military Command kept the definitely necessary and often bitter truth from their subordinate commands!

No doubt there are many things that both the political and military command of a state must keep secret. They are not suited to be common knowledge. On the other hand, however, a certain amount of truthful information among the higher commands, indeed, even down to the little front commanders, is required. This unvarnished information is one of the most vital foundations of reciprocal trust.

In Hitler's Germany, especially during the course of the war, it had come to the point that the technically flawlessly working propaganda had misled the trust of the general masses and abused them most grossly. This propaganda was so skillful and the general masses so gullible that the true context of our entire conduct of the war remained unknown to them right up to nearly the final moment. Undoubtedly that was not the case in the government offices and the higher military commands. Here, while one could not, indeed, form an entirely clear picture, one could evaluate large enough segments of the overall picture so that one could, with some certainty, draw conclusions about the whole.

Such a possibility was taken as given, at least after the year 1943. One must remember that every soldier and, additionally, every military commander is justifiably expected to reconnoiter things, especially the enemy, as exactly as possible so as to know how to act. Moreover, it must additionally be granted that in the thicket of lies of propaganda and press and often also from official reports from above, it was impossible to know the true state of things. Accordingly, the reconnaissance required here was not only forward against the enemy, but also to the rear, against *OKH*.

Under the pretext of increased security, Hitler had introduced a system into the German *Wehrmacht* that is best characterized by a saying coined at the front: 'Nobody is permitted to know his own mission.' This was a reaction to Hitler's well-known secrecy order. With the most nonsensical requirements for secrecy, a state of increasing confusion and ignorance within all military commands gradually developed. That suited Hitler's purposes perfectly, for that made it all the easier to conceal the true source of the innumerable mistakes and misfortunes, not least in the military area. That secrecy which was actually necessary was in no way improved by Hitler's secrecy requirements; rather it was negatively impacted.

In any case, in closing it must be stated that it was extremely difficult for the higher military commands, including the *Heeresgruppen*, to gain a clear picture even of their own area of command. Too much was concealed, distorted and falsified. Thus, out in the field one had to take matters into one's own hands and, as, indeed, the rules of military expertise demanded, try to gain a somewhat complete and clear picture of a larger sector of the big picture through close communications with one's neighbours. One attempted to do the same towards the rear. It was usually far more difficult to gain a clear picture over conditions, such as regarded armaments, the war-economy, replacements and the so-called 'Home Front' in general.

Even the Commanders in Chief of the *Heeresgruppen* and *Armeen* were quite inadequately informed in that respect and had to depend essentially upon opportune contacts of a personal nature. These, however, as already explained, could only be extremely incomplete. In the field I have often thought of the saying that we were artificially kept in the dark from above. That sounds like a joke, but contained a serious truth.

It must be made completely clear that foreigners, especially, but also the majority of all Germans, could not comprehend the inadequate orientation of the higher military commands and simply would not believe it. A *Feldmarschall*, for example, must know everything. Often, however, he knew less than the little Party *bonze* in the homeland. It is extremely difficult, today, when, at least in many areas, the cloud has been dispelled, to give anyone a true picture of the ever-thickening fog of lies, mistrust and propaganda that lay over everything. Many far more competent people than I can bear witness to the fact that things really were like that.

One cannot close these remarks without taking a position regarding the former well-known saying: 'If the *Führer* only knew, he would clear that up. But he is always lied to and deceived.' With this very simple saying people wanted to explain all the grievances and errors in the war and, especially, clear Hitler of the actual responsibility. The following must be added: First, the atmosphere of lies and grievances was created and ever thickened by Hitler, himself. Secondly, Hitler was the only man in Germany who had sufficient power to change and improve practically everything with one stroke of a pen. Finally, a dictator bears sole responsibility for the men whom he chooses for his closest colleagues and advisors. The selection of false advisors, the dismissal and elimination of useful and worthy men is entirely the doing of such self-willed men, no-one else.

The affair of 20 July [the failed assassination attempt] must also be seen from this viewpoint. If one knew the degree to which Hitler continually involved himself in details of the most ludicrous sort, then one could hardly assert that he overlooked or let himself be lied to about other vital and decisive things. He, himself, had constantly deceived himself and the German people. Every deception that was in accord with his own views was pleasant to him. Since the start of the Eastern Campaign, Hitler would only see and hear what agreed with his own extravagant plans. He was totally unconcerned with the degree to which these were fact or fiction.

Returning to the starting point of this discussion, it must again be stated that the *Heeresgruppe* received only inadequate information regarding the development of the situation in the west. Now, most suddenly, came the equally vague orientation from *OKH* regarding *Panzerarmee Wenck*. As mentioned above, this *Armee* was the decisive basis upon which Hitler based his denial of the *Heeresgruppe's* urgent request to pull back the 9th *Armee* before it was completely cut off by the enemy.

With great effort we succeeded in learning that the provisional command post of *Armee Wenck* was to be in Dessau. Both *General* Kinzel and I attempted to make telephone contact with the *Armee*. Only after many vain attempts did I succeed in getting telephone contact with *General* Wenck. The connection was so bad that I could only hear disconnected fragments. It was impossible get any usable information this way. Accordingly, we decided to send a general staff officer – it was *Oberst i.G.* von Harling – with a car to him. His assignment was to obtain exact figures on the spot regarding the strength, composition and intentions of this army and to inform *General* Wenck of the precise situation of *Heeresgruppe 'Weichsel'*, particularly of the 9th *Armee*, which he was to relieve. Von Harling drove off on about 18 April and returned the following day with the necessary information. It turned out to be precisely what the *Heeresgruppe* had feared. *'Panzerarmee Wenck'* was nothing more than a great bluff. The only question was whom it was to bluff? There were three possibilities:

1.) The enemy. This possibility must be excluded. Neither the Anglo-American nor Russian commands were that dumb.

2.) Our own military command, meaning *Heeresgruppen 'Schörner'* and *'Weichsel'* and Dönitz' staff. As the example of *Heeresgruppe 'Weichsel'* shows, the deception lasted barely 24 hours, or just long enough for us to determine the actual facts on the spot.

3.) The mass of the German people and the German soldier at the front. These were, in fact, the victims of their *Führer's* lies and his propaganda – here, probably, for the last time.

So far as I can retrospectively determine, the majority of the people and the troops believed with unshakable faith in this relief attack of *'Armee Wenck'* to relieve Berlin.

One can only gaze in amazement and horror at the suggestive power of Hitler's propaganda, even in this last minute, as, in truth, visible facts now truly gave the lie to all the German people against this propaganda. The people, however, awaited a 'miracle' where the raw truth and simple reason could not help but show total defeat to even the blindest.

Oberst von Harling presented a clear and factual account of what he had learned from *General der Panzertruppe* Wenck. The so-called *Panzerarmee* consisted of a force of thrown-together, newly-activated infantry and armoured formations of battalion and regimental strength that were assembled into so-called divisions, without having even the faintest resemblance to a genuine division, even on paper. So far as I remember, there was a total of about two so-called infantry divisions and about one *Panzer* division. The latter, however, had the strength of one reinforced *Panzerabteilung* [armoured battalion]. The figures on artillery, armour, etc. corresponded to this picture. All in all it was a thoroughly depressing outcome.

With this *'Armee'* the unfortunate *General* Wenck was to advance from the area southeast of Magdeburg both to Potsdam – Berlin to free the city, and also past Berlin on the south toward the Oder to link up with the 9th *Armee*.

As could have been anticipated, *Armee 'Wenck'* came neither to Potsdam – Berlin nor to the 9th *Armee*. This *Panzerarmee* found a not-so-glorious end in the area northwest of Berlin.

The *Heeresgruppe's* conception of the overall situation was fully confirmed by the hard facts regarding *Panzerarmee 'Wenck'*. For *Heeresgruppe 'Weichsel'* now it could only be a matter of making its final battle against all contrary orders from the bunker or from *OKH* in order to sacrifice the least possible German blood and allow the smallest possible number of German soldiers to fall into Russian hands. That meant, to put it simply, to conduct a fighting retreat so that the main body of the troops would finally fall into the hands of the Americans waiting in our rear. To attain that goal it still required bitter fighting to the end, especially against the Russians.

When you now sees these sentences written down before you it sounds very simple and uncomplicated. How difficult, however, this short and bitter stretch was to attain this objective!

Generaloberst Heinrici went to the Commander in Chief of the 9th *Armee* immediately following the return of the *Ic*. He intended to convince *General* Busse of the full severity of the danger threatening his *Armee* and to institute suitable measures to save this *Armee* at the last minute before it was cut off. *Generaloberst* Heinrici must have realized that, in so doing, he was acting contrary to Hitler's orders, which were also known to the 9th *Armee*, to hold fast at the Oder at any price. *General* Kinzel accompanied the Commander in Chief. I learned the results in a discussion that took place immediately after their return.

Their report made it evident that *General* Busse was just as clear about the untenable situation of the 9th *Armee* as was the *Heeresgruppe*. He shared the opinion that the *Armee* had to immediately start falling back to the west, avoiding Berlin, so as reach the area west of Berlin, there to link up with the 3rd *Panzerarmee*, thereby reestablishing a continuous front between the Elbe and Oder rivers. The Commander in Chief of the 9th *Armee*, however, wanted to have an order to that effect from Hitler. Although I was not present in person at the discussion with *General* Busse at the command post of the 9th *Armee*, I got the impression from the report of our Commander in Chief that he had tried everything to persuade *General* Busse of the necessity of immediate action, even without express orders to do so from Hitler, indeed, even contrary to Hitler's order.

After the discussion with the Commander in Chief, *General* Kinzel told me that he, too, had attempted in every way to convince *General* Busse, who was a friend of his. At present, however, both the Commander in Chief and also the Chief of the General Staff of the 9th *Armee* still held steadfastly to the senseless order to hold in place.

In the meantime the enemy continued his attacks in accord with his intentions described above. On 18 April the ring around the 9th *Armee* was practically closed. The 9th *Armee* now fought roughly in the general Oder line south of Fürstenberg – Oder-Spree-Canal – Fürstenwalde – Großer Wörther See – Schwielow See. Initially the *Armee* was most heavily attacked on its former front. Thus it could reposition only inadequate weak forces on its flank and rear. The *Armee* could, indeed, take advantage, there, of the numerous lakes. Later, however, that protection proved to be an extreme hindrance in the attempt to break out to the west.

In Berlin the Russians penetrated into the northern and eastern suburbs. There was already fighting near the Stettin and Silesian railway stations. The southern outskirts of Neukölln, Steglitz and Zehlendorf were already under attack. Bitter fighting raged around Potsdam, fighting that would completely destroy that old residence of the Prussian kings with its well-known architectural monuments.

The *Heeresgruppe* received constant reports from Berlin so long as any communications link was available with the city, and that still remained the case since the city was not yet entirely cut off, though the government quarter was already under attack. Granted, the

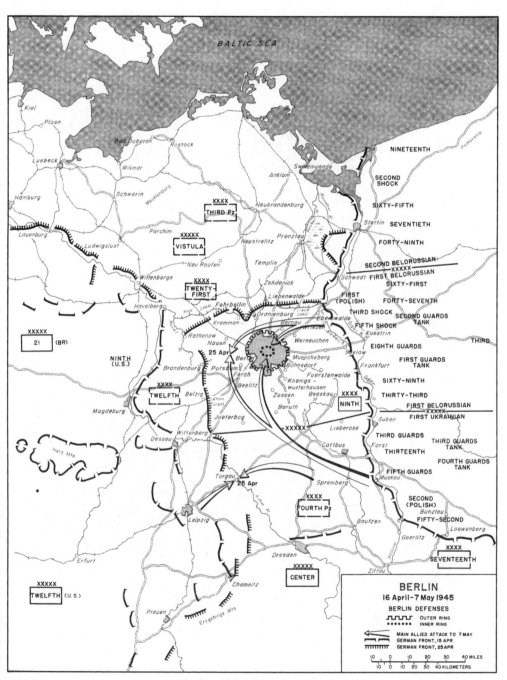

Berlin, 16 April–7 May 1945

General der Infanterie Kurt von Tippelskirch, CO 21. *Armee.* Tippelskirch briefly
relieved Heinrici of command of *Heeresgruppe 'Weichsel'* before the newly-appointed
replacement, *Generaloberst* Kurt Student, took over. (Bundesarchiv 101I-778-0015-35A)

Heeresgruppe could not itself take part in the battle, but it was still vital for it to know the state of the situation there. Conclusions could be drawn from the state of the battle in Berlin regarding further Russian intentions toward the Elbe.

The reports, most of which were situation reports passed on to me by *Oberst* Refior, the Chief of the General Staff of the Commandant of Berlin, had a dramatic ring and were nearly beyond belief: Heavy armoured fighting at the Alexanderplatz, enemy artillery fire on the Zoo Railway Station and the Kaiser Wilhelm Memorial Church. The first heavy-caliber artillery fire was falling on the Wilhelmstrasse and the new *Reichskanzlei*. Charlottenburg and Wedding were lost. The Russians had crossed the *Ostwestachse*.[1] One report pressed hard on the heels of another.

Although elements of a *Panzerkorps* of the 9th *Armee*, led by *General der Panzertruppen* Weidling had, apparently by chance, broken into the Berlin from the east and was now the heart of the resistance, the end was very fast approaching. Only in the government quarter did the fighting continue longer.[2]

In the 3rd *Panzerarmee* sector heavy Russian attacks opened against the entire length of the weakly-held Oder Front. Even on the first day the enemy gained several small bridgeheads across the Oder. The enemy attack from the south against the hastily constructed defensive flank along the Hohenzollern Kanal increased steadily. Here, too, came ever more numerous armoured forces.

Since, in the long run, it would be impossible for the 3rd *Panzerarmee* command to direct both the Oder Front facing east and, at the same time, the increasingly significant defensive front facing south, the *Heeresgruppe* initially formed and directly attached to itself a sort of *Armeegruppe*[3] commanded by *SS Obergruppenführer* Steiner with the staff of III *SS Panzerkorps*. That, however, could be no more than a temporary solution. A single *Korps* staff could not command this wide front that was provided with so few command-staffs.[4]

Accordingly the 21st *Armee* was formed. Its Commander in Chief was *General der Infanterie* von Tippelskirch. For his staff he received the remnants of the staff of the 4th *Panzerarmee* that had been withdrawn from East Prussia, with *Oberst i.G. Freiherr* von Varnbühler as Chief of the General Staff.

This new 21st *Armee* command took over the southern defensive flank of the 3rd *Panzerarmee* toward the end of April with three *Korps* staffs, as I remember, *Korps* 'Berlin' (formerly the north wing *Korps* of the 9th *Armee*), III *SS Panzerkorps* and VII *Panzerkorps*. The latter was a remnant *Korps* staff that had been brought out by sea from Gotenhafen shortly before the end of the 2nd *Armee*. I had the following revealing little

---

1   Translator's note – East-West Axis, a major east-west avenue dividing the city of Berlin, aligned with *Unter den Linden*, continuing in that alignment west of the *Pariser Platz* through *der Grosse Stern*.

2   Author's note – As I later determined, *General* Weidling had, in fact, received an order from Hitler through *General* Krebs.

3   Translator's note – An *Armeegruppe* was a force usually comprising one *Armee* and attachments – more than an *Armee* but less than a *Heeresgruppe*.

4   Translator's note – Note that this *Armeegruppe* was purely a command headquarters with no additional troops attached. It was to command troops already engaged in combat.

experience with the Commanding General of this *Korps*, *Generalleutnant* von Kessel, an old acquaintance from the difficult times in the battle for Siebenbürgen.[5]

Generalleutnant von Kessel reported to the *Heeresgruppe* at Hassleben immediately after his arrival from Gotenhafen. He was still feeling severely the effects of the bitter fighting on the Hela Peninsula.[6] He had been wounded and had the appearance that was common to grenadiers and even commanding generals who came out of *Kesselschlachten*, or 'pocket battles'. After he reported to the Commander in Chief and Chief of Staff he had a cup of coffee with me in my room, during which he told me about the last battle of the 2nd *Armee* in the Danzig area. In the course of the conversation he asked me for my own opinion regarding the general situation. I must have shown my astonishment and responded by asking him whether he could not, himself, answer that question from his recent experiences in the Danzig area. He replied that he thought we must be able to judge things more clearly here at the *Heeresgruppe*. Thereupon I answered, quite simply: "*Herr General*, the war is lost. Our fighting can, at best, only drag on for another two to three weeks. Then it is, finally, done. This battle now has only one justification, to save the main body of our troops and as much as is possible of northern Germany from the Russians. If the Western Powers today were to attack our rear from the Elbe, the end would come sooner and much bloodshed would be avoided."

That answer which, at the time seemed simple and to-the-point, appeared to hit the general harder than I would have thought possible. He simply could not and would not believe it. Even this man, who had been in a position to have had a certain perspective of at least the military situation and had just escaped the collapse of his own troops, apparently still hoped for a miracle.

---

5   Translator's note – Siebenbürgen (*lit.* 'Seven castles') originated as a mediaeval German settlement in Transylvania, now in Hungary and Rumania, starting in the 12th Century. The *Siebenbürger* colony retained its ethnic identity and solidarity through the Second World War and, despite mass emigration at the end of the war as ethnic Germans fled before the advancing Russians, primarily back to Germany, there are still significant ethnic German minorities in that area of Hungary and Romania.

6   Translator's note – The Hela Peninsula is a long sand-spit extending into the Danziger *Bucht* (Bay of Danzig) with the town of Hela at its extreme end.

Part XV

On his last visit to the 9th *Armee, Generaloberst* Heinrici had again telephoned *General* Krebs in Berlin and told him of the entire senselessness of leaving the 9th *Armee* in place. He closed with the strongest reproaches regarding the obvious deception with *Panzerarmee 'Wenck'*. The otherwise so calm, self-controlled man was excited and bitter as he spoke of the betrayal of the upstanding and courageous soldiers of the 9th *Armee*, who awaited a phantom that would relieve them. *General* Krebs was ice-cold and formal and only answered: 'The *Führer* relies upon the 9th *Armee*.' He went on to say that the *Herr General* Heinrici appeared to be misinformed about the actual possibilities of *Armee 'Wenck'*.

General Kinzel and I listened in on the conversation. *Generaloberst* Heinrici only looked at us, silently, and hung up without another word. Although his face twitched and worked, the Commander in Chief said, quite calmly, to us that he could no longer take part in this deliberate murder of the 9th *Armee*.

Following a brief discussion, *General* Kinzel was tasked with talking to the Chief of the General Staff of the 9th *Armee* and *General* Busse, to again clarify the present situation of the *Armee*. The *Armee* was then to receive orders from the *Heeresgruppe* to withdraw westward in the general direction of Potsdam at the earliest possible moment, starting tomorrow morning at the latest. Even if, as was most likely, the Russians had already completely closed the ring around the *Armee*, the *Armee* was to reverse its direction and attack with its main body toward the west and screen toward the east and south. In any event, enemy resistance was, at the time, least to the west. Every hour was precious before the Russians also increased their forces to the west. *General* Kinzel's conversation with the 9th *Armee* Chief of Staff and with the Commander in Chief of the 9th *Armee*, who joined in somewhat later, initially confirmed the *Heeresgruppe's* understanding that the *Armee* was now completely encircled. After some questions back and forth, which repeatedly dealt with the Hitler's inhuman order for the army to hold in place, *General* Kinzel communicated the *Heeresgruppe* order for an immediate fall-back to the west with the objective of attacking toward Wenck's weak forces.

Both the Commander in Chief and the Chief of Staff of the 9th *Armee* stressed that, in the present situation, an immediate withdrawal would be impossible. They apparently envisioned an orderly movement of the *Armee* as a whole. Both evaluated the situation such that, during the heavy fighting on the eastern and northern fronts, the necessary regrouping would have to take place by stages, the more so in that it involved inexperienced, newly-activated units in such a movement. Furthermore, the regrouping of the *Armee* played a major role. It must be conceded that the *Heeresgruppe* could not comprehend in detail the situation of the *Armee* as well as its Commander in Chief.

One thing, however, was certain. A forceful solution had to be sought and found, regardless of systematic planning. Just how difficult retreats are with inexperienced troops and how easy panic and confusion can begin we all well knew from experience. Nevertheless, here it was no longer just a matter of retreat, but of a forcible breakout to the west at any cost. The command of the 9th *Armee* was not yet ready to understand this. Knowing just what a clear, enterprising and energetic commander *General* Busse was, I could not quite understand his behaviour at that moment. We were wrangling with the *Armee* about carrying out an order that they had urgently requested from us for days. Granted, the situation was now incomparably more difficult, but an immediate breakout would have prevented much that had to come later if no action was taken.

The *Armee* command knew, however, that this order was issued by the Commander in Chief of the *Heeresgruppe* without endorsement by *OKH*. The *Heeresgruppe* had to painstakingly keep its order to the 9th *Armee* secret from *OKH*. Otherwise, in the last seconds, an insane counter-order would come, possibly with the elimination of the previous *Heeresgruppe* command. That, however, had to be avoided in the interests of about 100,000 soldiers.

The battle for the immediate withdrawal of the 9th *Armee* finally ended with agreement that *General* Busse would immediately make all requisite preparations and report to the *Heeresgruppe* when and how the withdrawal would be carried out. Again it must be pointed out that the command of the 9th *Armee* was in an extraordinarily difficult situation here. Withdrawal from the enemy would only be possible with heavy sacrifices and increasing pressure from an inexorable, closely-pursuing enemy. Nevertheless, it remained the only solution.

Right in the midst of this especially difficult situation for the *Heeresgruppe* command came the long-threatened change in Chief of the General Staff. *Generaloberst* Heinrici had not given up hopes that, after Hitler's decision to remain in Berlin, the plan for Dönitz' new command staff would be dropped. That, however, did not take place. Dönitz set up with his new staff in Eutin, and *General der Infanterie* Kinzel left us.

The not-unimportant question of his successor had, of course, already been pondered for some time both by the *Heeresgruppe* and by *OKH*. *General* Kinzel initially proposed that the present *Ia*, myself, should be his successor. The reasoning was that, despite youth and rank the present *Ia* was the one who had taken part in the command since the activation of the *Heeresgruppe* and, thus, best understood the overall situation. In addition, I possessed his complete trust and, he believed, also that of the Commander in Chief. Commander in Chief, Chief of Staff and *Ia* were in basic agreement in our understanding of the situation and of what now remained to be done. He promised a fruitful cooperation with the *Heeresgruppe* as Dönitz's future Chief of General Staff.

When *General* Kinzel explained his plan to me it was completely clear to me that *OKH*, especially *General* Krebs, would never accept this solution. The First General Staff Officer of *Heeresgruppe* 'Weichsel' (this author) had, in his short term of service, made himself entirely too unpopular. The innumerable great and small conflicts would never be forgotten. *OKH* could hardly be blamed for having the idea that I was, conceivably, the most unsuitable man for the position.

Nevertheless, the proposal was made and, as expected, rejected. On its side, *OKH* proposed *Generalmajor* von Trotha, at that time Chief of the Operations Section [*Operationsabteilung*] as Chief of the General Staff of the *Heeresgruppe*. He was not unknown to *Generaloberst* Heinrici, since he had already been his Chief of the General Staff at the 4th *Armee*, if only for a short time. He was not initially enthusiastic about the proposal of Trotha, and said to *General* Kinzel, in my presence: 'Trotha may be smart and clever, but he is a complete visionary. I know him.'

Nevertheless, Trotha was named as *General* Kinzel's successor. For me this solution was not very pleasant. *General* Trotha and I knew each other quite well and each knew that, in general, we were of opposing viewpoints. That was hardly the most promising basis for fruitful cooperation between the Chief of the General Staff and the First General Staff Officer.

He had, for a long time, been *Ia* of *Heeresgruppe 'Süd'* when I was *Ia* of the 6th *Armee*. At that time major differences of opinion developed between us concerning the situation, especially during the fighting in Rumania which led to the second total defeat of the 6th *Armee*. It was due to Trotha's unfounded super-optimism that the Command of *Heeresgruppe 'Süd'* stood by without doing a thing while the catastrophe developed.

Trotha was a clever, decent officer, but he never had his feet upon the earth, meaning upon the solid footing of sober facts. Trotha was characterized by great, high-flying, generally fantastic plans which took no account of the sober givens of the actual situation. He presented his opinions with a great deal of zest and elegance. He was also nimble enough to modify his presentation according to the situation. Thus, after a short guest-performance as Chief of the General Staff of the 4th *Armee* he finally became Chief of the *Operationsabteilung*. Probably he was following in the wake of his old commander, *General* Wenck.

Even in the first telephone conversation that I had with him in his new role, our strongly contradictory outlooks resurfaced. For every factual and unpleasant report, he always had an optimistic interpretation and, basically, attempted to gloss over the thing. His basic viewpoint – or, at least, this is what he repeatedly told me – was that, despite all difficulties, there were still many new possible ways to achieve final success. He was one of those men who simply would not accept the inevitable end.

For these reasons I considered it my duty to report to *General* Kinzel that, from my side, he could hardly count on a trusting cooperation with *General* von Trotha in the best interests of the *Heeresgruppe*. On these grounds, despite the serious situation, I requested that I be transferred. *General* Kinzel fully understood that my request was not for personal, but for more practical reasons. My request for replacement was turned down by *Generaloberst* Heinrici. He required that, despite the predictable difficulties with *General* von Trotha, I remain, and assured me that I would continue to have his complete trust and understanding.

In the final analysis, the Commander in Chief was probably right, in the existing situation and from his viewpoint. However, it was unavoidable that the Commander in Chief came to depend increasingly on the *Ia* and that the Chief of the General Staff came to be in a somewhat isolated and not very fortunate position. That, too, I had seen in the offing and, in the general interest, and not least also that of von Trotha, wanted to avoid.

Although I respected him as a person, from the first day that he performed his new official duties there was considerable tension between us. It was impossible for me to listen uncritically to this unbounded, strongly pushed, expedient optimism. My suspicion was not unfounded that *General* von Trotha had been sent to *Heeresgruppe 'Weichsel'* very much on purpose. Obviously, what *OKH* viewed as the dark defeatism of this *Heeresgruppe* command was, finally, to be put in order by the 'in-spite-of-everything' emphatic optimism of a reliable and devoted man from *OKH*. One often got the impression that *General* von Trotha saw that as his primary duty and mission.

It was obvious that he had brought strict instructions with him from *General* Krebs to influence the command of the *Heeresgruppe* in accord with the views of Hitler and *OKH*. Even though, now that he was on the spot with the *Heeresgruppe*, he could better evaluate the true situation than before, when he was in the *Operationsabteilung*, he did not want to face the facts.

The 9th *Armee*, now completely cut off, was attacked from all sides and increasingly compressed. Our only link was by radio. An attempt to establish contact using the 'Storch'[1] failed. Thus was the fate of what was, under the circumstances, the strongest and most combat-worthy *Armee* of the *Heeresgruppe,* sealed.

The *Armee* was too late in its decision to break out. In the midst of an ever-narrowing area filled with refugees and civilians, in the bloodiest and most desperate fighting, a brave troop, energetically lead, initially put everything into breaking out to the west. It was impossible to supply the *Armee* with ammunition, fuel and rations. The *Heeresgruppe* received but few reports. The tighter the *Kessel* became, the fewer the radio transmissions, since the *Armee* did not want to reveal itself. Nearly completely smashed and wiped out, elements of the *Armee* managed to break through to the west under the command of its Commander in Chief.

In closing this sad chapter it must be stated that, yet again, an *Armee* had been senselessly sacrificed to no good avail. In this case, moreover, it is astonishing that Hitler did not, as one would have expected, at least, use the 9th *Armee* for the defense of Berlin instead of leaving it to be destroyed before the gates of the city. Still, it may be that he no longer cared to further postpone his own end.

In any case, it would have been of inestimable value to the *Heeresgruppe* if it had even succeeded in withdrawing the 9th *Armee* from the Russian grasp long enough to make possible a surrender to the western enemy. In my own opinion, during the last four weeks it became exclusively a matter of sparing German blood and saving our troops from Russian captivity. For that objective, only, could and must bitter fighting still be demanded from the troops.

As the 9th *Armee* had to be written off and hopes based on *General* Wenck proved to be a delusion, Hitler ordered *Heeresgruppe* 'Weichsel' to concentrate 'strong forces', attack Berlin from the north, and relieve the city. Its other tasks, namely defense of the Oder and the Hohenzollern Canal remained in effect. This order arrived at the end of April from *OKH* out of Rheinsberg. At that moment it appeared that *Feldmarschall* Keitel, or, better said, *Generaloberst* Jodl, had taken over supreme military command. These orders got to those strategists by radio from the *Führer* bunker, where these insane ideas and last feverish fantasies, edited by *General* Krebs, were flashed out through the ether. Orders of this sort poured forth in quick succession, revoking each other and never making real sense. All in all they gave the impression only that those who were cut off in the bunker felt pressed to order something, anything, no matter how senseless, in hopes that something might come of it.

It must be stated again that Jodl, even Keitel, knew very well that all these orders were senseless and, at that point in time, were yet more criminal than before. The *Heeresgruppe* had just lost an *Armee*. It was committing its last strength in a bitter defensive battle

---

1   Translator's note – *Fieseler 'Storch'*, a small liaison plane famous for its ability to land and take off from short strips.

at the Oder River and Hohenzollern Canal. The Russians had already breached both obstacles at numerous places. The fragile continuity of the front could be torn asunder at any moment. In that case the frazzled and, for the most part, combat-inexperienced troops of the 3rd *Panzerarmee* and 21st *Armee* would scatter like chaff in the wind.

General der Panzertruppen von Manteuffel had clearly and soberly judged the condition of his army to be just about that. The new Commander in Chief of the 21st *Armee*, *General* von Tippelskirch, was most cautious in his judgement. He gave the impression that he did not want to mess things up with either *OKW* or the *Heeresgruppe*. That was unequivocally his position in the later removal of *General* Heinrici.

The new mission, attack to relieve Berlin, was just as impossible for the *Heeresgruppe* to carry out as the previous one. The *Heeresgruppe* could not defend its current front of about 200 kilometers with the wholly inadequate forces of the 3rd *Panzerarmee* and 21st *Armee* – all in all, on a purely numerical basis, these were estimated to amount to about five or six divisions. There were no reserves, nor was there one single usable armoured formation left. On the Oder Front, as, also, at the Hohenzollern Canal, the Russians had attained deep penetrations that could no longer be eliminated, nor even sealed off. The enemy picture – unclear as it was for the *Heeresgruppe* due to inadequate reconnaissance – still revealed that the Russians intended a thrust from the area northwest of Berlin generally northward toward Mecklenburg.

An operation of the sort proposed threatened to cut off the *Heeresgruppe*, whose deep south flank was completely open and, at the time, hung in the air west of Oranienburg. In this situation Hitler and *OKH* demanded an attack to recapture Berlin.

The *Heeresgruppe*, for its part, requested that, in light of this new assignment and the menacing danger of encirclement, a withdrawal to the line Neuruppin – Neustrelitz – Neubrandenburg – Anklam. The request was refused. The Oder was to be held. In actual fact, it had already been lost.

III *SS Panzerkorps*, commanded by *SS Obergruppenführer* Steiner was tasked with the relief attack on Berlin. The order went to him directly through *OKW* and Jodl, himself, was with Steiner. In this case the *Heeresgruppe* and the 21st *Armee*, which was commanding there, had simply been bypassed. All that was left to the two commands was the confirmation and execution.

SS Obergruppenführer Steiner immediately expressed his reservations. On the other hand, he started to carry out the orders. *Generaloberst* Heinrici immediately went to be present on the spot. When he returned he was extremely depressed. Should the *Heeresgruppe* permit itself to be cut off and destroyed by the Russians like the 9th *Armee*? Hitler's order in that regard was clear and unequivocal, and Jodl and Keitel sat in Rheinsburg to watch over this order suspiciously. At that time they sent their unoccupied general staff officers out from *OKH* and *OKW* on an assembly line basis around the *Heeresgruppe* area to keep track of what was actually happening. This sudden curiosity about our intentions was well-founded. At this point Rheinsburg was pretty close to the front. One could never know. It was best to carry out one's own reconnaissance to determine the right time to move the headquarters.

Generaloberst Heinrici called *General* von Trotha and myself to him and instituted another evaluation of the situation. The results were simple enough: If the *Heeresgruppe* carried out the orders as issued, then, within a few days, it would go the same way as the 9th *Armee*. There could no longer be any talk of both defending at the Oder and relief of Berlin. The Commander in Chief then called, first on the Chief of the General Staff, and then on me to state our opinions. *General* von Trotha expounded a longer evaluation. After some backing and filling regarding the simple facts this evaluation finally culminated by saying that the *Heeresgruppe* must do its utmost to carry out the order of *OKH*. He said next to nothing about the 'how'.

My reply to the Commander in Chief was rather brief. I had to agree with the judgement of the Commander in Chief at every point. Accordingly, the only possible decision for the *Heeresgruppe* was to operate contrary to the *OKW* orders in order to save our troops from the Russians. My proposal was, starting immediately, to fall back to the west to the Ücker River-line. Furthermore, to make all preparations for, as the final objective, withdrawal to the Mecklenburg lakes and to form the shortest possible line there between the Baltic and the Elbe. There we must hold as long as possible until, probably, the general surrender would take place.

In these measures I saw the only possibility to accomplish something useful in the present situation. In response to the Commander in Chief's question as to what to do in the event that the Russians cut us off first, I answered, 'Break through to the west.' If, however, we acted immediately I did not think that this extreme case was at all likely.

Hardly had the words, 'general surrender' dropped when *General* von Trotha excitedly burst forth and said there could never be any talk about a surrender. Since *Generaloberst* Heinrici remained silent and merely looked at me, I answered that it was extremely obvious that it would come to a surrender. That had been true in the military histories of all peoples when there was no other possibility. If I remember correctly, I then referred to Blücher's surrender at Ratekau.[2]

General von Trotha objected strongly to any thoughts of surrender and also to the suggestion to fall back to the west without orders from *OKW*. In response to the Commander in Chief's brief question as to what he then proposed, he could only say to attempt everything possible to carry out the orders as given. His honor as a German officer was mentioned repeatedly in this discussion.

In closing *Generaloberst* Heinrici said roughly the following: 'Here it is no longer a matter of fine words and feelings, but of bloody earnest. At this point I can no longer take responsibility for carrying out this senseless, suicidal order. Not one more German soldier should be uselessly sacrificed. This is the responsibility I have to my soldiers, my people and a power higher than Hitler.' Despite further protests of the Chief of Staff the Commander in Chief essentially agreed with my evaluation. *General* von Trotha requested and received permission to visit the 1st *Marineschützen-Division* at the front.

The Commander in Chief then discussed the necessary details for the unequivocal decision to withdraw with the *Heeresgruppe* to the west against *OKW* orders. He wanted to discuss this thing himself with the two Commanders in Chief of the *Armeen*, not for

---

2   Translator's note – In the course of the disastrous Prussian campaign against the French in 1806, Blücher was forced to surrender at Ratekau the remnant of the Prussian army he had led away when the main body capitulated at Prenzlau. When Blücher surrendered at Ratekau he demanded that surrender document include a clause stating that he only surrendered due to lack of provisions and ammunition and that his soldiers be honoured by the French. Bound only by his word of honour, he was soon exchanged and went on to enjoy a spectacular career that made him one of Germany's all-time military heroes.

his own reassurance, but to establish completely clear understandings and to take all responsibility on himself.

In order to be able to carry out this intention without immediate hindrance from *OKW* it was necessary that our daily situation report to *OKH* be suitably imprecise. The fact that – despite all the liaison officers that *OKH* and *OKW* had sent out – the frontal situation was extremely unclear was very useful to the *Heeresgruppe*. Since the *Ia* was responsible for these reports, I had to edit them appropriately. Even though any imprecision in reports is greatly to be avoided in war – things had gradually developed otherwise respecting the *OKW* reports from above – there was no other alternative here. If Keitel and Jodl had realized in time what was happening with the *Heeresgruppe*, they would have done all in their power to give us over to encirclement and destruction by the Russians, as Hitler had ordered. The correctness of these suspicions would later be proven by the removal of the Commander in Chief.

Part XVI

In the meantime, the Russians had forced the *Heeresgruppe* back on the entire Oder Front. The front now ran along the Ücker River. The Hohenzollern Canal had also been crossed by the Russians in its entire extent. The attack of III. *SS Panzerkorps* toward Berlin – it consisted, I believe of three battalions and a few tanks – had bogged down completely. As the battle for Prenzlau began, the Commander in Chief decided to move the command post. We moved the command section [*Führungsabteilung*] to a small rural estate near Waren. From there, despite the massive Russian superiority in forces and the extremely difficult command situation, the *Heeresgruppe* directed a relatively orderly withdrawal to the Mecklenburg lake plain.

The 21st *Armee*, to the south, was to conform to the above movement and attempt, by a suitably phased withdrawal of its southern wing, to gradually establish contact with the Elbe River. In the course of this fighting, *OKW – OKH* in Rehinsberg was now, as mentioned above, surprised by the Russians despite all its own reconnaissance. Judging from eyewitness reports, the decampment to Eutin must have been a bit sudden. The *Heeresgruppe* had, indeed, given timely warnings, but *Generaloberst* Jodl apparently wanted to set an example. He had blamed the *Heeresgruppe* for being over-hasty in moving its command post to the Waren area and said that the move was much too far.

On the journey to the new command post I came upon a *Hitler-Jugend* battalion near Hohenlychen. The youths – their average age was about 14 years old – made a fresh, disciplined, good impression. Only their armament and the far-too-heavy packs failed to seem suitable for them. Actually, the sight of them had to bring a blush of shame to the face of any soldier. Things had gone so far that children were being sent into battle. The battalion commander gave me some information about their ages and degree of training. What I heard was sad. Despite all their courage and youthful enthusiasm for the adventure, for that especially excited these youths, it was a crime to send these children against a battle-hardened enemy. No state-government has the right, when they are at the end of their rope, to sacrifice the under-age youth of their people for their own mistakes. That is interfering with the biological foundation of the people in a way that can never be justified by any exaggerated and false conception of honour. These youths could accomplish nothing more for the honor of their people. Defending that honor would become their duty when they finally became men.

On the day of the flight of *OKW* from Rheinsburg, Keitel and Jodl apparently clearly realized that the combat conduct of *Heeresgruppe* 'Weichsel' was not in accord with their, meaning Hitler's, orders. Various reports by their reconnaissance officers revealed that the *Heeresgruppe* front was already much further to the west than they had realized. Possibly *Feldmarschall* Keitel and Jodl had uncovered details that they were not yet meant to know when they visited the 21st *Armee*, shortly before their departure for Eutin.

Feldmarschall Keitel called the Commander in Chief in the morning of 26 April 1945, accused him of disobedience and unsoldierly weakness and closed by declaring that, effective immediately, he was relieved of his position. Until his successor was named, *General der Infanterie* von Tippelskirch, the commander of the 21st *Armee*, was to command the *Heeresgruppe*. He, Keitel, would come that very day to the command post of the *Heeresgruppe* to call it to account and finally put an end to the *Schweinerei*.[1] We could expect him.

Unfortunately I did not listen in on this conversation. *General* von Trotha did so and was completely taken aback by it and told me about it. *Generaloberst* Heinrici remained calm and collected. Shortly thereafter *Generaloberst* Jodl called. In his icy, impersonal fashion he told *Generaloberst* Heinrici about the same as what Keitel had said, only this essentially younger *General* could not forebear from sharply attacking in personally offensive and dishonourable fashion our Commander in Chief, who, one could well say, had grown gray in honourable service,

This conversation used words like cowardice, weakly incompetent command and the like. Additionally, Jodl declared that the Chief of the General Staff was also relieved, effective immediately. As for the *Ia*, who had knowingly made false reports, he would be attended to later. The entire command of the *Heeresgruppe* was worthless. From the very outset they had been worthless. That must finally be changed. He concluded by ordering *Generaloberst* Heinrici to report as soon as possible to *OKW* in Eutin.

As I listened in on this incredible conversation cold rage arose in me. The fact was that precisely these two men – who had just given such overwhelmingly convincing proof of their capability to perform responsibly and of their high military capabilities as Hitler's most trusted military advisors, as was so beautifully shown and were, at that very moment, in flight to the last hiding-hole in the *Reich* – wanted, at the last second, to prevent a just, upright, greatly-respected officer from accomplishing what, above everything, still needed to be done: namely, while maintaining the honour of the German soldier, to save his troops from senseless destruction.[2]

After the conversation I implored the Commander in Chief that, under no circumstances, should he give up his command of the *Heeresgruppe*, but that, on the contrary, he should continue to lead the *Heeresgruppe* despite these absurd orders. Under any and all circumstances the *Armeen* would continue to obey his orders. I described to him how a change-of-command in this situation could only result in serious detriments for our troops. Keitel and Jodl would attempt by every means, according to the old principles of staying in place and holding to the last man, to put the *Heeresgruppe* in the hands of the Russians. That must, at all costs, be prevented. Moreover, at this point neither *OKH* nor *OKW* had the power to haul him out of the *Heeresgruppe*. Every upstanding officer and soldier, as well as his staff and also the attached troops would stand up for that at any time.

I proposed that *Feldmarschall* Keitel be arrested upon his arrival at the *Heeresgruppe* and put in protective custody to insure that there was no more stupidity from him, and as a pledge-of-good-faith against Jodl.[3] He [Heinrici] should remain and continue to command the *Heeresgruppe* as before. The officers of the command section

---

1   Translator's note – Probably best left at exactly what it says in German, i.e. 'swinery', disgraceful and disgusting behaviour.
2   Translator's note – I left this as the original, lengthy, run-on sentence because that truly expressed the author's sense of utter disbelief and outrage.
3   Translator's note – Or, perhaps better put, as a hostage to insure Jodl's future conduct.

Generalmajor Erich Dethleffsen, Chief of Staff of *Heeresgruppe 'Weichsel'*
28 April-May 1945. (Bundesarchiv 146-1984-116-19)

[*Führungsabteilung*] and a special *Kommando* of reliable soldiers of the 3rd *Panzerarmee* were available to serve as protection against any sort of gangster attempts against his person, with which, judging by known example, one had to reckon. The latter had been promised and assured for some time in the event of the extreme case, in discussions I had engaged in, without knowledge of my Commander in Chief, with *General der Panzertruppen* von Manteuffel and his Chief of Staff and *Ia*.

Generaloberst Heinrici was too deeply disturbed by these events coming hard on each other's heels to be able to come to an immediate decision regarding his person. He wanted to talk with the Commanders in Chief of the *Armeen* and review the matter again. In the meantime I instituted appropriate security measures for our little command post and immediately called the 3rd *Panzerarmee*.

General von Manteuffel was not there, so I spoke with the Chief of the General Staff and *Ia*. They were equally embittered about the removal of the Commander in Chief, and expressed similar conviction that the Commander in Chief should remain in command of the *Heeresgruppe*. They assured me that this would also be the attitude of their Commander in Chief and promised me that they would immediately start the above-mentioned *Kommando* on its way to us. The commander of this *Kommando* would report to me. He and his soldiers would execute any order, even when it was against the personalities of *OKH* or *OKW*.

This may well read like a Karl May romance or back-step novel and yet it was, at the time, in bloody earnest. All means were justified to prevent further interference in our military command. Only that point of view justified such an indubitably extraordinary action.

Although everything was prepared, it did not come to any acts of violence, since *Feldmarschall* Keitel chose to drive immediately to Eutin and *OKW* did not send anyone to arrest the Commander in Chief. Nevertheless, we remained armed for whatever might happen.

At about noon our Commander in Chief again discussed all the possibilities with *General* von Trotha and myself. He had resolved to carry out *OKW* orders, since he believed that it was no longer possible for *OKW* to interfere effectively in the command of the *Heeresgruppe*. On the one hand, he was convinced that the *Armeen* would act in whatever way was best for their troops. In addition, he believed that a general surrender was immediately imminent.

This being the case, he was no longer needed. Anyone could do what was needed. He believed that he had done his duty for his troops. Despite repeated attempts both by the 3rd *Panzerarmee* and myself to persuade him to remain in command, *Generaloberst* Heinrici remained firm in his decision.

Late in the afternoon of that same day I had to accompany him to the command post of the 21st *Armee*. The command post was in a little village southeast of Müritz, whose name I have forgotten. *General* von Tippelskirch awaited us in a small fisherman's house. He had been informed of the situation directly by *OKW* and was already provided with a new mission for the *Heeresgruppe*. The new Chief of the General Staff for the *Heeresgruppe* was *Generalmajor* Dethleffsen, former Chief of the *Operationsabteilung* in the General Staff of the *Heer*. The change of command was brief. *General* von Tippelskirch expressed his extreme personal regrets over this course of events and assured *Generaloberst* Heinrici how unpleasant and painful it was for him, even temporarily, to relieve him. He had pondered the matter, forward and backward, at length and been unable to come up with any practical solution. I got the feeling here that *General* von Tippelskirch was not being entirely open. Doubtless it would have been easy for him to decline the temporary appointment by *OKW*, justifying his refusal with reference to the especially difficult situation of his own *Armee*. Certainly *General der Panzertruppen* von Manteuffel would have done so. The agreement between the *Heeresgruppe* command and the *Armee* commanders over the only possible conduct of the battle, even contrary to orders from above was here, in my opinion, broken by the Commander in Chief of the 21st *Armee*, regardless of all contrary excuses. *Generaloberst* Heinrici also perceived it that way.

When the formalities of change of command were completed, *Generaloberst* Heinrici declined the proffered hospitality and took his leave of *General* von Tippelskirch and *General* Dethleffsen. He then turned to me and, for the last time, I stood eye-to-eye with my Commander in Chief, whom I had learned to respect to the highest degree in the short time in which I had the honor of serving under him. His eyes and his handshake said more to me than words could have. I then accompanied him to his car and asked him again, under no circumstances, to go to *OKW* at Eutin, but, instead, to go to the 3rd *Panzerarmee*, where he was already expected.

I still greatly feared that *OKW* would cover this honourable old soldier at the last minute with insults and shame. Accordingly I urgently entreated his personal *Ordonnanzoffizier*, *Rittmeister* von Bila, to go to the 3rd *Panzerarmee*, no matter what. He promised to do so.

Part XVII

The new Chief of the General Staff, *Generalmajor* Dethleffsen, was only known to me by name as a particularly gifted and competent officer. He had been chief of general staff at both *Korps* and *Armee* level. As we got to know each other at the command post of the 21st *Armee*, I received the impression of an extremely nervous and badly over-worked man. During the short time of our reciprocal cooperation this impression strengthened. *OKW* demanded that the new *Heeresgruppe* command unconditionally hold in a general line that was advanced as far east as possible toward the Oder. The only possible such line at that point was the approximate line of the Elbe at Wittenberge – Mecklenburg Lakes – Stralsund.

This line, however, was neither particularly favorable in its natural course – aside from the lakes – nor in any way fortified, and, all-in-all, much too long to be defended in its entirety. There was no alternative but to fall back by stages farther to the west. Both the 3rd *Panzerarmee* and the 21st *Armee* reported ever declining combat strength. Everywhere there were gaps. There was no way of building a continuous front. Thus the Russians daily broke through the thin lines of both armies, and often it was only with difficulty that the troops could withdraw in some sort of order to save them from encirclement, destruction and captivity.

Some now believe that this was more or less disordered flight. That is not correct. Granted, here and there were indications of what was more flight than retreat, but, all-in-all, it must be stated that the troops at the front remained in contact with the enemy and fought so skillfully, despite all their inferiority, that the main body of the *Heeresgruppe* was finally overrun by the Anglo-Americans from the rear and captured by them. In any case, as the new command of the *Heeresgruppe* took over, despite *OKW's* orders to hold, the Russians broke through the north wing via Greifswald and Stralsund to Rostock. In the south the situation was totally obscure and, despite dispatch of numerous *Ordonnanzoffiziere* was never really clarified. There the Russians must also have broken through to Parchim.

On 28 April 1945 the *Heeresgruppe* moved its headquarters to the barracks in Güstrow. The city of Güstrow, itself, was a picture of incredible confusion of refugees and troops of every sort of mostly rear-area services. When I arrived there – the Commander in Chief and Chief of Staff had driven ahead – I was greeted by the leader of the communications services with the fact that there was no contact with either the 3rd *Panzerarmee* or the 21st *Armee*. Accordingly I had several radio messages sent to both *Armeen*.

There was, of course, contact with *OKW*. They called immediately and wanted to know something about the situation. Unfortunately there was nothing I could say, since, as stated, there was no contact of any sort. This remained the case throughout the entire day. We learned nothing at all from the 21st *Armee*. *General* von Tippelskirch, who had been with the 3rd *Panzerarmee*, brought some rather imprecise reports back with him. Naturally, things were no better for the *Armeen* with their contact to *Korps* and divisions.

Therefore one could only feel one's way around in the dark. Only now and again did an officer who had been sent out on reconnaissance return with a report, and, given the speed at which the action was moving to the west, most of those had already been overtaken by events. Even the sparse radio messages – several came from the 3rd *Panzerarmee*, the 21st *Armee* persisted in stubborn silence – could no longer provide a clear picture.

The following day – it was 1 May 1945 – the staff of the *Heeresgruppe* had to make another change of position, since Güstrow was already under attack by Russian armour. The staff and the command section [*Führungsabteilung*] moved to a small rural estate, *Gutshof Schoenwalde*, between Schwerin and Gadebusch. The *Oberquartiermeisterabteilung* [logistics section] went to Schwerin.

On this journey it was evident that here the Anglo-American air force ruled the skies. Continual attacks on all roads and byways by low-flying aircraft were the norm. At this command post, too, there was again only radio contact with *OKW/OKH*. Accordingly I immediately had radio messages sent out to 21st *Armee* and 3rd *Panzerarmee*. However, after some time the leader of the communications service reported to me that the 3rd *Panzerarmee* had reported, but not the 21st *Armee*.

Regarding the 21st *Armee* we did not, at that time, even know the location of its command post. Two days prior its intention had been initially to go to the vicinity of Parchim and then to Ludwigslust. After one general staff officer and two additional *Ordonnanzoffiziere* were already underway to determine the location and situation, we hoped, shortly, to get some information. As noon approached I suddenly got radio contact with the *Ia* of the 3rd *Panzerarmee*, *Oberst i.G.* Ludendorff. He had just returned from the front and arrived at the new command post of the *Armee* in Schwerin. The Commander in Chief and Chief of the General Staff of the 3rd *Panzerarmee* were still en route. He could not provide a precise situation report.

The *Armee*, too, had practically nothing but radio contact with its *Korps* and divisions. Generally one or another of the Commander in Chief, Chief of Staff and *Ia* were on the road to learn what the situation was on the spot. According to his report the 3rd *Panzerarmee* was, at that time, fighting approximately on the line of the lakes, Plauer See [lake] – Goldberg – Sternberg.[1]

At the southern wing of the 3rd *Panzerarmee* the Russians had broken through at the narrow stretch of land between two of the lakes at Karow[2] and were advancing toward Parchim. The 3rd *Panzerarmee* had no contact with the 21st *Armee* and also knew nothing of its situation at the time. He presumed that the 21st *Armee* was southwest of the Plauer See.

Apparently there was a large gap at the northern wing of the 3rd *Panzerarmee*, or, better said, that wing hung in the air southwest of Rostock. In any case, the Russians had taken Rostock and were advancing along the coast with armour toward Wismar. Unconfirmed reports said that they were already in Wismar. That would shortly be confirmed.

This last report was very disturbing in that the Russians could also advance further to Lübeck and come between us and their Western Allies. Accordingly, defense of the sector between the Großer Schweriner See and Wismar assumed decisive significance.

---

1   Translator's note – There is a line of numerous small lakes extending roughly northwest from the Plauer See near Alt-Schwerin past Sternberg.
2   Translator's note – Just northwest of Alt-Schwerin.

Generaloberst Kurt Student, final commander of *Heeresgruppe* *'Weichsel'*. (Bundesarchiv 183-L19500)

The 3rd *Panzerarmee* was just as clear regarding that as we were. It had, therefore, done its utmost to throw into that endangered location all the forces that it could possibly scrape up. However, nobody could say what the situation there was.

As soon as he concluded, I immediately reported this unpleasant and extremely imprecise news to *OKW* and, at the same time, asked about the situation in Schleswig – Holstein, meaning, in our rear. I learned only a very small amount, actually only that, at the time, *Armee Busch* was engaged in heavy fighting with the Americans in the area north and northeast of Hamburg.

As for my question of what the *Heeresgruppe* should actually do if the Americans attacked our rear, which was to be expected at any time, they could offer neither advice nor an answer. As I spoke with *OKW* the door of my room opened and *Generaloberst* Student and an *Ordonnanzoffizier* walked in. He was the third Commander in Chief that *Heeresgruppe 'Weichsel'* received at the eleventh hour.

After listening to my report he delivered a greeting from my wife. To my astonishment he told me that, the night before last he had been in quarters in the house of my parents-in-law in Barsinghausen near Hannover[3] and had met my wife. During the night he had been forced to flee before American armour. He had crossed the Elbe just in time and was now to assume command of *Heeresgruppe 'Weichsel'*.

That afternoon *General* von Tippelskirch turned over command of the *Heeresgruppe* to *Generaloberst* Student. At the situation briefing called for on that occasion, which *General* Dethleffsen delivered and at which I also had to be present, I was astonished by one thing after another. It was amazing what a clear picture of the situation our Chief of the General Staff had. The numerous uncertainties were passed over.

Generaloberst Student asked a great many questions, but, despite his recent experiences, seemed to believe that the *Heeresgruppe* now had to 'finally' go over to the defensive between the Elbe River, Schweriner See and the coast. Nothing was said of the Americans in our rear. They seemed not to exist. I was somewhat astounded at the optimism of the three exalted gentlemen.

That evening, one on top of the other, came reports of Hitler's death, Dönitz's succession, Hitler's testament etc. Everyone else sat with the Commander in Chief at the loudspeaker. I remained in my room since I was awaiting contact with the 3rd *Panzerarmee* and also had some other work to do. My *Ordonnanzoffizier* finally brought in a small radio and thus I, too, heard Hitler's swan-song.

During that night numerous orders arrived from *OKH* regarding immediate transmission of this rather long announcement to the troops. The announcement came in endless teletypes. I had no idea how this thing was to be delivered to the troops at the front line in the current situation. That, however, was required.

The Chief of the General Staff, whose nerves had, apparently, continued to suffer, yelled at me in response to my question regarding that matter, saying that I, as *Ia*, was to organize these simple matters. He couldn't do everything himself.

Now, where the 21st *Armee* now was, which simply meant the staff of that *Armee*, we still did not know. Since *OKH* expressly demanded written transmission of the announcement by hand of officers, I had the entire thing duplicated during the night and, in the early hours of the morning, sent a vehicle to the 3rd *Panzerarmee*.

---

3   Translator's note – Barsinghausen is located about 20 kilometers west of Hannover.

In the meantime that *Armee* had informed me that they had already, so far as possible, passed the news on to the troops. The following morning the *Heeresgruppe* again had no contact at all with the two *Armeen*. Probably both headquarters had changed location and, in the press of circumstances, had not so reported.

Finally a radio message from the 21st *Armee* arrived, the first report in three days. It came from III *SS Panzerkorps* and contained the following: Immediate swearing in of the troops. The previous *Fahneneid* [oath of loyalty] was null and void. Thus emerged an interesting, if also, in the current state of things, completely trivial legal problem.

The entire *Wehrmacht* had sworn its oath of loyalty personally to Hitler. He was now dead. He had appointed Dönitz as his successor. Thus, the troops must actually be immediately sworn to this man. Accordingly, the order for swearing the loyalty oath to Dönitz should have arrived at the same time as the announcement. That had not happened.

We were not concerned with such questions. Aside from III *SS Panzerkorps*, apparently nobody had thought of that question. It was never clarified and, two days later, was rendered moot by the capitulation.

Generaloberst Student and the Chief of the *Heeresgruppe* General Staff wanted to drive to both *Armeen* on this second day of the new Commander in Chief's command. I was just concerning myself with establishing contact with the 3rd *Panzerarmee* when a call suddenly came in.

Oberst Voigt, the staff officer for the *Heeresgruppe* artillery reported on the telephone. He was in a village about three kilometers distant. He briefly informed me that he was, even as he spoke, a prisoner of the Americans. So the Americans had finally arrived. Apparently they were not about to allow their dear allies to come all the way to Hamburg. Today the Russians could halt just before Lübeck.

In response to my question as to how *Oberst* Voigt, as a prisoner, could still telephone, he told me that nobody paid any attention. American officers were present in the same room. Since most of our motor vehicles were en route to that village for reasons of protection from air attack, I asked *Oberst* Voigt to immediately set our motor vehicles in motion. Perhaps that would still work. He promised to do so.

My *Ordonnanzoffizier* had listened in on our conversation. He was ordered to see to the motor vehicles and, at the same time, to also determine whether the Americans were already here. From outside came the typical sharp bark of tank guns. When we stepped to the window we saw American tanks, which were firing somewhere in the area, approaching on the road from Gadebusch. Since our manor house was in the midst of a small park, about two kilometers from the main road, we could hope that it would, initially, as be overlooked. That was how things turned out.

I wanted to report these newest events to the Commander in Chief and Chief of Staff. En route I ran into them, ready to depart, in the entrance hall. They received my report and then I asked regarding further intentions and orders. In passing I was ordered to attempt to get to the command post of the 21st *Armee* as quickly as possible with the most necessary elements of the command section. *Generaloberst* Student and the Chief of the General Staff wanted to get there first. From there the command of the *Heeresgruppe* could continue to function. My question about the command post of the 21st *Armee*, whose whereabouts had been unknown for three days, was answered as follows: It must be near Ludwigslust.

I therefore asked for confirmation that I should initially drive to Ludwigslust. That was affirmed. As for my question about how to get there, which was a most practical matter, I was told: Swing to the north via Bad Kleinen. That called for some discussion, for I had received a reliable report from an *Ordonnazoffizier* that the Russians were already there. My proposal was to go through the Americans, crossing the main Gadebusch – Schwerin road and driving to Ludwigslust on byways. The gentlemen were, however, in a hurry and wanted to be off.

The Chief of the General Staff took me aside and told me that a *'Storch'* would stand by for me until 1500 hours at a well-concealed airstrip. If we did not get away in good time, under any circumstances I must attempt to fly to Eutin with the *'Storch'* in order to report the situation of the *Heeresgruppe* to *OKW*. Then the Commander in Chief and the Chief of the General Staff drove off. Long after the surrender I learned from the newspaper that *Generaloberst* Student had been captured in southern Germany. I never learned what happened to the Chief of the General Staff.

My mission was clear and unequivocal; but it no longer made any sense. There could no longer be any talk of further direction of the *Heeresgruppe*. On the other hand, however, it made no difference where one was captured by the Americans, whether it was here or anywhere else. In the meantime, a considerable disturbance was evident in the house. Everyone ran every which-way and began to pack.

So I had the section leaders of the individual sections and the headquarters commander come and initially issued the necessary orders for moving the headquarters. For my journey into the unknown I would take only what was most necessary. All the others were ordered initially to drive to Lübeck under command of the headquarters commander and then, if possible, to Eutin. It was important here to keep the individual groups and vehicles together so that they could go into captivity as an organized group.

At about 1400 hours I drove off with the first group, which was to accompany me to Ludwigslust. There were four motor vehicles. Only half an hour later, the *Ic, Oberst i.G.* Von Harling, was to follow. He, too, had about four or five motor vehicles and a motorcycle messenger. The Americans still had not come to our manor house.

After a rather exciting drive in the midst of the American troops my little group was captured. *Heeresgruppe 'Weichsel'* had ceased to exist. The war appeared to be over. It is no accident that I used the word 'appeared', For two years later, as I write this report, we still have no peace.

Appendix: Order of Battle
Heeresgruppe 'Weichsel'[1]

Command positions
Oberbefehlshaber:
Reichsführer-SS Heinrich Himmler (24 January – 20 March 1945)
Generaloberst Gotthard Heinrici (21 March – 29 April 1945)
Generaloberst Kurt Student (30 April – May 1945)

Chef des Generalstabes:
Generalmajor der Waffen-SS Heinz Lammerding (24 January – 21 March 1945)
General der Infanterie Eberhard Kinzel (21 March – 22 April 1945)
Generalmajor Ivo-Thilo von Trotha (22 – 28 April 1945)
Generalmajor Erich Dethleffsen (28 April – May 1945)

1. Generalstabsoffizier (Ia):
Oberst i.G. Hans-Georg Eismann (24 January – May 1945)

April 1945 Order of Battle *Heeresgruppe 'Weichsel'*

III SS 'Germanic' *Panzerkorps*
11 SS 'Nordland' PzGrD
23 SS 'Nederland' PzGrD
27 SS 'Langemarck' GrD
28 SS 'Wallonien' GrD
503 SS sPzAbt

3. *Panzer-Armee*
Oberbefehlshaber: General der Panzertruppen Hasso von Manteuffel
Korps '**Swinemunde**'
402 ID
2 MD

XXXII *Korps*
'Voigt' ID
281 ID
549 VGrD
Stettin Garrison

Korps 'Oder'
610 ID
'Klossek' ID

XXXXVI *Panzerkorps*
547 VGrD
1 MD

9. *Armee*
Oberbefehlshaber: General der Infanterie Theodor Busse
156 ID
541 VGrD
404 VAK
406 VAK
408 VAK

---

1   Established 24 January 1945.

CI *Korps*
5 JD
606 ID
309 'Berlin' ID
25 PzGrD
KGr '1001 Nights'

LVI *Panzerkorps*
9 FJD
20 PzGrD
'Müncheberg' PzD

XI SS *Panzerkorps*
303 'Döberitz' ID
169 ID
712 ID
'Kurmark' PzGrD
502 sSSPzAbt

Frankfurt an der Oder Garrison
V SS *Gebirgskorps*
286 ID
32 SS '30. Januar' GrD
391 SD
561 SS PzJAbt

Key to abbreviations:

FJD – *Fallschirmjäger* Division; GrD – *Grenadier* Division; ID – *Infanterie* Division; JD – *Jäger* Division; KGr – *Kampfgruppe*; MD – *Marine* Division; PzD – *Panzer* Division; PzGrD – *Panzergrenadier* Division; PzJAbt – *Panzerjäger Abteilung*; SD – *Sicherungs* Division; sSSPzAbt – *schwere SS Panzerabteilung*; VAK – *Volks-Artilleriekorps*; VGrD – *Volksgrenadier* Division.

GLOSSARY OF MILITARY TERMS[1]

Abteilung: When referring to cavalry, armoured or artillery commands, it is equivalent to a battalion. In other contexts it can be a tactical detachment or unit or an administrative section or department.

Aufklärungs-:   Reconnaissance

Freiherr: Baron

Führerhauptquartier :   *Führer* Headquarters

Gau: District

Gauleiter: District leader [a powerful Nazi civilian official]

General des Transportwesens: General Staff Officer in charge of the transportation system.

Heeresgruppe :   Army Group

Ia: 1st General Staff Officer (operations)

Ib: 2nd General Staff Officer (logistics)

Ic: 3rd General Staff Officer (intelligence)

Kessel :   Pocket. I prefer to retain the German *Kessel* when referring to encirclements on the scale of Stalingrad, Falaise, Kurland, East Prussia and Pomerania.

Kleinkampf, Kleinkrieg: Guerilla warfare

Kriegsakademie: War college

Kriegsmarine: Navy

Luftwaffe: Air Force

Mitteln: Means

Ordonnanzoffizier :   Special-missions staff officer

Pak: Anti-tank gun

Panzer: Tank

Panzerfaust: The *Panzerfaust* was a recoilless disposable lightweight one-man anti-tank weapon firing a large hollow-charge grenade. Later models increased the range from 30 to 100 meters, the armour penetration from 140 mm at 30° to 200 mm at 30°. A portion of the gases from the propellant charge in the disposable firing tube vented to the rear to eliminate recoil. These made conspicuous the firing position of the operator and created a danger zone behind the weapon.

Panzergrenadier: Armoured infantry rifleman, [mechanized] infantry

Panzerjäger: Member of anti-tank unit or tank-destroyer vehicle

Panzerjagdkommando,Panzerjägerkommando: Troops of selected volunteers, armed with *Panzerfäuste* and machine pistols, mounted on bicycles. Formed as a measure of desperation in response to the lack of armoured vehicles as the war drew to an end, these troops were a credible threat to enemy armour in

---

1   Added by translator.

favorable terrain and built-up areas, but could not, in any way, substitute for the missing armour.

Pionier: Pioneers, combat engineers

Sonder-:   Special

SPW, Schützenpanzerwagen: Lightly armoured half-tracked personnel carrier, some mounting infantry support weapons such as mortars, rocket launchers, light anti-aircraft or the short-barrelled 7.5 cm gun.

Schwerpunkt :   Point of main concentration, a German term that has now entered the entire world's military vocabulary.

Staffel: Squadron, 9-12 aircraft.

Stuka: Dive bomber

Volkssturm: A home-guard under party leadership, the last *Volkssturm* consisted of a levy of half-trained civilians ranging in age from 16 to 60 years of age, poorly armed and essentially without military equipment. Sometimes dismissed and sent home by merciful military commanders, they did, on occasion, prove that they knew how to die for their homes and loved ones.

Werfer, Nebelwerfer: *Nebelwerfer* were rocket launchers, not guns or mortars. Although laying smoke screens and delivering chemicals were among their original capabilities, the abstention from the use of poison gas in WWII led to the rapid development of high explosive projectiles, and the primary mission of the *Nebelwerfer* batteries became delivering massive volumes of high explosive rounds with powerful blast effect or incendiary-oil projectiles and also laying smoke screens.

Holes around the rim of the *Turbine* plate at the base of the solid-fuel rocket motor drilled at an angle to the axis of the rocket caused it to rotate rapidly, stabilizing it in flight. Because the spin-stabilized rocket projectiles for the *15 cm NbWf 41* had the rocket motor in front, the high-explosive payload in the rear, and detonated when the nose struck the ground, the bursting point was elevated above the ground surface, giving a devastatingly effective fragmentation and blast effect. Salvos from an entire battery of multiple-tube *Nebelwerfer* bursting over an area in rapid sequence gave waves of high and low pressure that, in the early Russian campaigns, resulted in discovery of many enemy dead with no visible signs of external injuries, their lungs apparently burst by the extreme pressure differential.

A 15 cm *Werfer-Abteilung* (battalion), with its three batteries of 6 launchers each, could deliver a salvo of 108 rounds from its 18 launchers in 10 seconds, followed by successive salvoes on the same target at 80-90 second intervals, giving 5 salvoes in 5 minutes. The 15 cm rockets came in both high-explosive and smoke rounds. Larger rockets had the rocket-motor in the rear, the bursting charge in the front. The 21 cm *Werfer-Abteilung* could deliver 90 rounds (18 launchers at 5 tubes each) in 10 seconds, with one salvo every 2.5 minutes, giving 3 salvos in 5 minutes. The 30 cm *Werfer 42 Abteilung* could deliver 108 rounds in 10 seconds, with 3 minutes between salvos, giving 3 salvoes in six minutes. The *28/32 cm Werfer 41 Abteilung* could deliver 108 rounds in 10 seconds, with five minutes between salvos.

Because, even after the switch from black-powder to smokeless propellent reduced the massive smoke-trails of the rockets, the clouds of dust raised by the exhausts of the rockets in the launching area made it easy for the enemy to rapidly identify the location of launching sites, standard practice was to launch a few rapid salvos, laying down a sudden, massive application of high explosive saturating an area, then immediately change positions to avoid retaliation.

Thanks to the relatively light weight of the launchers, they could move over terrain that would not support conventional artillery and could be shifted around by manpower or almost any powered vehicle.

21 cm rockets were only made in high-explosive. 28 cm rounds were high-explosive, 32 cm were *Flammöl* (incendiary). 30 cm rockets were high-explosive only. Because of the sound of the rockets in flight, American troops in Normandy dubbed them 'Screaming Meemies', the British, 'Moaning Minnies'.

The name *Nebelwerfer* was taken over from the 10 cm *Nebelwerfer 35*, which was a true 'trench mortar' employed by the *Nebeltruppen* for laying smoke screens. After 1940 the *Nebel-Abteilungen* gradually converted from mortars (*Werfer*) to rocket launchers, such as the six-tube electrically ignited breech-loading rocket launcher, the 15 cm *Nebelwerfer 41*, which retained the 'smoke mortar' designation for reasons of deception. There were *Nebelwerfer Brigaden* consisting of two *Nebelwerfer* regiments and separate *Nebelwerfer* regiments. Regiments included three *Abteilungen* (battalions) of three batteries each. There were also independent *Abteilungen*. There were *Abteilungen* of the 15 cm six-tube *Nebelwerfer 15 cm-41*, five-tube *21 cm Nebelwerfer 42* and of the 28/32 cm *Nebelwerfer 41*, which was a carriage mounting frames for six rockets, either the 32 cm *Flammöl*, incendiary, rockets or, with inserts, the 28 cm high-explosive rockets. The heavy 28 and 32 cm *Wurfkörper* could be launched from their wood or metal packing boxes either separately or arranged on simple frames or racks.

From the very start, all *Nebeltruppen* were motorized. The final organization of the *Nebeltruppe* in World War II was as independent *Nebelwerferabteilungen (mot.)*, *Werferregimenter (mot.)* and *schwere* [heavy] *Werferregimenter (mot.)*. The independent *Nebelwerferabteilungen* were capable of employing smoke rounds, gas rounds or (for limited missions) high explosive rounds. Their *forte* was, aside from firing gas rounds, in the ability to provide smoke coverage rapidly and for extended periods (several hours) and over extensive areas. Effective in the spring of 1943, a *Werferregiment (mot.)* consisted of two *Abteilungen* of 15 cm *Nebelwerfer* and one *Abteilung* of either 30 or 21 cm *Nebelwerfer*. A *schwere Werferregiment (mot.)* consisted of two *Abteilungen* 30 cm *Nebelwerfer* and one *Abteilung* of either 15 or 21 cm *Nebelwerfer*.

Panzer-Pioniere, the combat engineer companies of *Panzer* divisions, had half-tracks with six individual launching racks, three on each side, for launching the heavy rockets.

The *Panzer-Werfer 42* (15 cm) consisted of ten tubes in two superimposed rows of five mounted on a very lightly armoured *Maultier* half-track, the armour merely providing splinter protection and protection against the exhaust of the rockets. Between the armour (8 mm on body, 10mm on cab) and the rocket-launcher, the vehicle was overloaded, resulting in breakdowns. However, the half-track mount permitted rapid position changes.

The *SS* developed an 8 cm multiple-track launcher with 24 double-rails firing fiin-stabilized 8 cm rockets. Although a successful design, production factors prevented general introduction.

The 30 cm *R-Werfer 56*, introduced in the closing months of the war, no longer carried the deception-designation, *Nebelwerfer*, but the word *Raketen* was still not written out. With inserted rails, it could also fire the 15 cm and 21 cm rockets.

The range of the rockets was only half or less than that of artillery and the rockets were ineffective against point-targets, concrete or armoured emplacements or structures. The mission of the rocket troops was strictly defined as application of sudden, massive concentrations of fire on area targets, whereas the missions of artillery was to deliver fire against point targets, deliver harrassing fire and final protective fire (blocking barrages), as well as rolling barrages in front of attacks. *Nebelwerfer* were not effective in any of these roles. Dispersion of the rockets prevented employment against point targets or in close proximity to friendly troops, thus excluding final protective fire close to friendly positions. Because of the dispersion of rockets, the launchers were to be used in *Abteilung* (battalion) or larger groupings, in which case the areas targeted would be saturated with impacts. The launchers were not intended, nor were they effective, for use as individual weapons. Availability of the precious ammunition was always limited, so employment was always limited, concentrated in both time and area. *Nebelwerfer* were never to be employed for missions that could be accomplished by division artillery.

Artillery shells have to withstand the high pressures of the propellant gasses in the gun-barrel and the sudden acceleration, which determine minimum wall thicknesses, limiting the space available for the bursting charge. Rockets are accelerated over a longer period of time by their own motors, allowing far thinner walls and a far greater bursting charge in relation to projectile weight. Since the launchers consisted of open tubes or racks that merely aimed the rockets, and did not have to absorb recoil, the projectors were inexpensive to produce and the tubes did not wear out as rapidly as rifled artillery tubes. Optimum range for the 15 cm rockets was between 4000 and 6500 meters, for the 21 cm rockets between 5500 and 7850 meters. The large rockets had extremely short ranges, the 28 cm between 750 and 1925 meters, the 32 cm between 875 and 2200 meters. The 30 cm *Nebelwerfer 42* was a six-rocket rack on a wheeled carriage, similar to the 28/32 cm *Nebelwerfer 41*. Its rocket was developed to improve on the extremely short range of the earlier heavy rockets and had an effective range between 800 and 4550 meters, with a minimum possible range of about 500 meters.

Glossary of alternative place names

Third Reich era	Modern equivalent
Arnswalde	Choszczno
Berlinchen	Barlinek
Bromberg	Bydgoszcz
Crössinsee	Krössinsee
Deutsch-Krone	Wałcz
Elbing	Elbląg
Graudenz	Grudziądz
Kolberg	Kołobrzeg
Küstrin	Kostrzyn
Marienburg	Malbork
Marienwerder	Kwidzyn
Medue	Madue
Neustettin	Szczecinek
Posen	Poznań
Schneidemühl	Piła
Stettin	Szczecin
Thorn	Toruń

Bibliography[1]

Bender, Roger James & Hugh Page Taylor, *Uniforms, Organization and History of the Waffen-SS,* R. James Bender Publishing, San Jose, California, 1969–1982, 5 volumes.

Buchner, Alex, *Das Handbuch der Deutschen Infanterie, 1939 – 1945,* Podzun Pallas Verlag, Friedberg, 1987. Although there is an English translation of this, the English translation is flawed by serious and substantial errors in translation.

Emde, Joachim, *Die Nebelwerfer: Entwicklung und Einsatz der Werfertruppe im Zweiten Weltkrieg,* Podzun-Pallas Verlag, Dorheim, 1979.

Engelmann, Joachim, *Deutsche Raketen-Werfer,* Podzun-Pallas-Verlag, Dorheim, 1977.

Gander, Terry and Peter Chamberlain, *Weapons of the Third Reich: An Encyclopedic Survey of All Small Arms, Artillery and Special Weapons of the German Land Forces, 1939 – 1945,* Doubleday and Company, Inc, Garden City, New York, 1979.

Höhne, Heinz, *Der Orden unter dem Totenkopf, die Geschichte der SS,* Reinhard Mohn OHG, Gütersloh, 1967. English language edition, *The Order of the Death's Head,* Ballantine Books, New York, 1971. The English language edition is invaluable as a source of English language terms for the exhausting array of departmental titles and designations in the world of Himmler's SS.

Le Tissier, Tony, *Der Kampf um Berlin, 1945, von der Seelower Höhen zur Reichskanzlei,* Ullstein, Frankfurt/Main, 1991. The original version in English was titled *The Battle of Berlin 1945,* published by Jonathan Cape, London 1988. I happened to use the German language version, which has minor differences.

Le Tissier, Tony, *Durchbruch an der Oder, der Vormarsch der Roten Armee 1945,* Ullstein, Frankfurt/Main, 1995. The original version in English was *Zhukov at the Oder.* I happen to prefer the German edition which differs in some details.

Magenheimer, Heinz, *Abwehrschlacht an der Weichsel 1945, Vorbereitung, Ablauf, Erfahrungen, Einzelschriften zur militärischen Geschichte des Zweiten Weltkrieges,* Verlag Rombach Freiburg, 2nd revised edition, 1986.

Murawski, Erich, *Die Eroberung Pommerns durch die Rote Armee,* Harald Boldt Verlag, Boppard am Rhein, 1969.

Paul, Wolfgang, *Der Endkampf um Deutschland,* Bechtle Verlag, Esslingen am Neckar, 1976.

Philippi, Alfred and Ferdinand Heim, *Der Feldzug gegen Sowjetrußland, 1941–1945,* W. Kohlhammer Verlag, Stuttgart, 1962.

Rielau, Hans, *Oberstleutnant a.D., Geschichte der Nebeltruppe,* Hergestellt bei ABC – und Selbstschutzschule im Auftrag BMVtdg fü H IV 1, Köln 1965.

Sawinski, Rolf, *Die Ordensburg Krössinsee in Pommern, von der NS-Ordensburg zur polnischen Kaserne,* Helios Verlags- und Buchvetriebsgesellschaft, Aachen, 2004, 2008.

---

1 *Oberst i.G.* Eismann wrote from his personal recollections. There was no bibliography attached to his notes. The following bibliography includes references that the editor found most useful in understanding the events *Oberst i.G.* Eismann describes.

Schäufler, Hans, *1945 – Panzer an der Weichsel, Soldaten der letzten Stunde*, Motorbuch Verlag, Stuttgart, 1979.

Tessin, Georg, *Verbände und Truppen der deutschen Wehrmacht und Waffen SS im Zweiten Weltkrieg 1939 – 1945*, Biblio Verlag, Osnabrück, 1974, 2. Auflage, 18 volumes.

Tieke, Wilhelm, *Das Endkampf zwischen Oder und Elbe, der Kampf um Berlin 1945*, Motorbuch Verlag, Stuttgart, 1981.

Tieke, Wilhelm, *Korps Steiner, Nordland – Nederland, Nachträge zu den Truppengeschichten*, Kameradenwerk Korps Steiner e.V. 1987. Also available translated into English by F. P. Steinhardt – see next entry.

Tieke, Wilhelm, *Tragödie um die Treue: Kampf und Untergang des III. (Germ.) SS-Panzer-Korps*, Nation Europa Verlag GmbH, Coburg, 4th revised edition, 1996. This is also available, translated into English by F. P. Steinhardt as *Tragedy of the Faithful*, JJ Fedorowicz, Winnipeg. This edition also includes Tieke's '*Korps Steiner*'.

Ziemke, Earl F., *Army Historical Series, Stalingrad to Berlin: The German Defeat in the East*, Office of the Chief of Military History, United States Army, Washington D.C., 1968.

Related titles published by Helion & Company

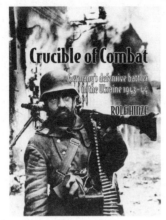

Crucible of Combat. Germany's defensive
battles in the Ukraine 1943-44
Rolf Hinze
504pp, photos, maps
Hardback
ISBN 978-1-906033-39-2

After Stalingrad. The Red Army's Winter
Offensive 1942-1943
David M. Glantz
536pp, photos, maps
Hardback
ISBN 978-1-906033-26-2

A selection of forthcoming titles

Barbarossa Derailed. The Battles for Smolensk, July-August 1941
David M. Glantz   ISBN 978-1-906033-72-9

Entrapment. Soviet Operations to Capture Budapest, December 1944
Kamen Nevenkin   ISBN 978-1-906033-73-6

A Flawed Genius. Field Marshal Walter Model, a critical biography
Marcel Stein   ISBN 978-1-906033-30-9

HELION & COMPANY
26 Willow Road, Solihull, West Midlands B91 1UE, England
Telephone 0121 705 3393   Fax 0121 711 4075
Website: http://www.helion.co.uk